WALKING
with
FRIENDS

WALKING
with
FRIENDS

*An Inspirational Year
on the PGA Tour*

D. J. GREGORY

with Steve Eubanks

SSE

SIMON SPOTLIGHT ENTERTAINMENT
New York   London   Toronto   Sydney

Simon Spotlight Entertainment
A Division of Simon & Schuster, Inc.
1230 Avenue of the Americas
New York, NY 10020

First Simon Spotlight Entertainment hardcover edition May 2009

SIMON SPOTLIGHT ENTERTAINMENT and colophon
are trademarks of Simon & Schuster, Inc.

For information about special discounts for bulk purchases,
please contact Simon & Schuster Special Sales at 1-866-506-1949
or business@simonandschuster.com.

The Simon & Schuster Speakers Bureau can bring authors to your live event.
For more information or to book an event, contact the Simon & Schuster Speakers
Bureau at 1-866-248-3049 or visit our website at www.simonspeakers.com.

Designed by Dana Sloan

Manufactured in the United States of America

1   3   5   7   9   10   8   6   4   2

Library of Congress Cataloging-in-Publication Data

Gregory, D.J., 1978–
Walking with friends : an inspirational year on the PGA tour /
by D.J. Gregory, with Steve Eubanks.
p. cm.
1. Golf—Tournaments—United States—Anecdotes. 2. PGA Tour
(Association)—Anecdotes. 3. Golfers—United States—Anecdotes.
4. Gregory, D.J., 1978– —Anecdotes. 5. Cerebral palsied—United States—
Anecdotes. I. Eubanks, Steve, 1962– II. Title.
GV970.G77 2009
796.352'66—dc22   2009005692

ISBN-13 978-1-4391-5403-8
ISBN-10   1-4391-5403-1
ISBN-13 978-1-4391-5623-0 (ebook)
ISBN-10   1-4391-5623-9 (ebook)

❖   ❖   ❖

This is for my family and friends. Thank you for
all of your love, support, and encouragement.
I appreciate all the hard work that went on
behind the scenes to make my incredible year a reality.
Your support and encouragement made it possible,
and I hope everyone enjoys reliving this journey.

CONTENTS

CONTENTS

FOREWORD

Don't we all wish we could lay claim to an incredible journey? Almost everyone has, at one point or another, dreamed of an epic voyage, living out a long-held fantasy, or accomplishing something you thought was beyond your ability. Unfortunately, too few of us follow through with those ambitions. Our dreams remain locked in a prison of self-doubt, suppressed by procrastination until one day we wake up and realize that "Someday, I'll . . ." is never going to come.

Well, friends, it doesn't have to be that way. For the better part of twenty years, I have had the privilege of knowing someone who proved to me that if you want something bad enough, no matter how great the odds, you can find a way to make your dreams come true. That person is D.J. Gregory.

I first met D.J. when he was just a kid. My booth mate and old pal, Ken Venturi, took an interest in the young boy on crutches who showed up at the base of our tower several times a year. Kenny showered young D.J. with kindness and eventually invited him to come up and watch some golf from the comfort of our makeshift studio. For several years after that, D.J. would watch the action from our broadcast booth, listening in on a spare headset, his face full of wonder and excitement. You could almost see the wheels of his mind spinning. It was obvious that D.J. loved everything about the PGA Tour. To him, professional golf was a romantic, chivalrous way of life.

As the years marched on, D.J.'s love for the PGA Tour continued to grow. We would see him out at various tournaments, always smiling and finding a way to put smiles on the faces of those around him.

His love of golf and infectious personality made his incredible journey seem almost inevitable, even though when it finally happened, it was, in my opinion, one of the greatest stories and greatest feats of the year.

Sure, some people say nothing could top Tiger Woods's epic U.S. Open victory over Rocco Mediate, while others point to Padraig Harrington's back-to-back major wins at the Open Championship and the PGA. But for me, D.J.'s performance was far more dramatic. And with all due respect to Tiger's victory walk on wounded knee, there is no comparison to the adversity D.J. Gregory has had to overcome.

Watching D.J. walk can sometimes be painful. How, you wonder, does a man with cerebral palsy manage to do the routine things we take for granted in life? And yet, D.J. gets along fine, enjoying every minute of every day and bringing joy to those he encounters. When he first came up with the idea of walking every round of every event on the PGA Tour for an entire season, I thought it was an ambitious goal, and I wasn't sure if D.J. knew what he was getting himself into. But I knew his heart and spirit, and I knew that if anybody could pull this off it would be D.J. I know he credits me with helping him get started on his journey, but my role was almost too trivial to mention. It was D.J. who realized he could live his dream by doing something no one had ever done, and it was he who touched everyone who encountered him along the way.

It was wonderful to watch his legend grow by the week. Every local paper ran a profile on him. Fans began to follow D.J. instead of the players, and many approached him for autographs before, during, and after his rounds.

D.J. walked a thousand miles to reach his goal. Sometimes he fell, but he always picked himself up and proudly made it to the finish line. I am thrilled this story is being told. We can all learn something from D.J., his perseverance, dedication, and indomitable spirit. By the end of his yearlong odyssey, D.J.

had become the darling of the PGA Tour, a friend to the players and a hero to the fans.

I am proud to know him. And once you read his story, I'm confident that you will be proud to know him, too.

—*Jim Nantz*
Westport, Connecticut

CHAPTER ONE

"I'VE GOT AN IDEA"

Sometimes I have to pinch myself. Could I really be this lucky? Not only do I have the love and support of a great family; I am an entrepreneur who has experienced the thrills and perils of being self-employed and I'm in great health. I am eternally grateful for all those things. But that's not why I feel so privileged; that's not why, over the course of one extraordinary year, I woke up every morning laughing and shaking my head, knowing that I had to be the luckiest man alive. During an eleven-month stretch, beginning the first full week of January and going through the second week of November, I lived out a dream that would turn every die-hard sports fan green with envy. Even when my year was all but over, I would look at myself in the mirror and ask: Is this really happening? Am I really doing this?

The "this" was travel with the PGA Tour, not just to an event or two, but to all of them. From the first event of the year on the island of Maui through the season-ending tournament at Disney World, I lived out a sports fantasy unlike any other. Every week of the PGA Tour, I traveled to a golf tournament where I walked every round with the greatest golfers in the world, many of whom I am fortunate enough to call my friends.

On a crisp November Sunday in Orlando, my journey came to a close. I had walked every round of every event, a total distance of almost a thousand miles. As I walked around the back of the eighteenth green and toward the scorer's trailer, one of the first people to speak to me was Rich Beem, the man who had danced his way into history when he'd held off Tiger Woods to win the 2002 PGA Championship.

"Congratulations," Rich said as we hugged. "I'm proud of you."

It was hard to respond to that. Having someone who makes his living grinding out shot after shot in one of the most demanding sports ever invented, a pro I had admired for years, tell me he was proud of me was overwhelming. My voice caught as I thanked Rich, not just for his kind words but for his friendship.

Davis Love III also congratulated me, which was more than a little ironic since Davis had just won the Children's Miracle Network Classic at Disney World. It was Davis's twentieth career win, a milestone that earned him a rare lifetime exemption on the PGA Tour, meaning he could never lose his card for the rest of his life. It also got him back into the Mercedes-Benz Championship, the tour's "tournament of champions," an early-season event reserved for the previous year's winners. Disney was his first win since 2006 and only his second since 2003, so Davis and his family were thrilled to be returning to

Maui. The fact that he would take a moment to congratulate me was a little overwhelming.

You'd think I would have been used to it. I had been on the receiving end of congratulatory hugs for the better part of a month, starting at the Tour Championship presented by Coca-Cola in late September. That tournament, held every year at East Lake Golf Club in Atlanta (the home club of Bobby Jones), was the finale of the season-long FedEx Cup, and the last time I would see a number of players. Some of the friends I'd made—guys like Kenny Perry, who became an unlikely Ryder Cup hero at age forty-eight, and Camilo Villegas, who won that week at East Lake—made a point of finding me and wishing me well. Kenny put an arm on my shoulder and said, "You're my hero. God bless you, man."

Words can't describe the feeling you get when a man you have looked up to for years, as I have looked up to Kenny, calls you his hero. I felt humbled and wholly undeserving.

After all, these were the guys who hit the shots;

these were the players, the globe-trotting athletes who pounded 300-yard drives and sank 10-foot putts for a living. These were the men who earned their paychecks by making cuts, the real stars of the PGA Tour. All I did was walk around and watch them. Granted, I walked a lot. A thousand miles is no small feat; in fact, it would be like walking from Midtown Manhattan to Daytona Beach, Florida. But I never had to hit a single shot, make a single putt, or post a single score. I walked, and I watched, which was all I'd ever wanted to do.

Unlike a lot of other golf fans, I never had any ambition to play professionally, even as a kid. I never saw myself standing on the eighteenth green with a putt to win the Masters. I never even thought about being a ranked amateur. Nor did I ever consider being a tour caddie, a profession that attracts some of the game's most colorful characters. Even though I love sports, and hold a master's degree in sports management, those jobs were not just outside my consciousness, they were beyond my abilities.

You see, I am one of 760,000 people in America who have cerebral palsy.

Thirty years ago I was born ten weeks premature. My lungs were not fully developed, and during my time in the neonatal intensive care unit nurses put too much oxygen into my body, which burst the capillaries in my brain that control my lower extremities. As a result, I have a noncontagious, nonprogressive disorder that affects my motor centers.

I have trouble controlling my feet and legs, and I don't walk like everyone else (unless by everyone you mean an eighty-year-old guy with two broken hips), but I get along fine. It was a tough break. I had to have surgeries just so I could separate my legs. I also had five eye surgeries, because I was born cross-eyed. No big deal. Some premature kids have long-term respiratory problems; some have learning disabilities; some who end up with cerebral palsy can't stand or speak; and some are incapable of feeding and caring for themselves. I was fortunate enough not to have any of those problems. I just walk with a cane.

I feel lucky to be able to walk at all. When I was an infant, my parents were told that I would probably spend my life in a wheelchair. In addition to my legs contorting so that my feet almost pointed backward, my toes stacked on top of each other until my feet were taller than they were wide. It took five surgeries to straighten my legs out enough for me to stand. But that didn't stop me from being mobile. I started belly crawling at age two and refused to slow down. Even with my legs in casts or braces I figured out a way to move. Once the surgeries were completed and I was able to get up on my feet, I quickly learned how to get around with a walker, one of those aluminum support devices you see at nursing homes and hospitals. Before my parents knew it, I was moving so fast they had to put wheels on the frame. From there I progressed to crutches, then two canes, and finally, after years of practice and thousands of falls, I got to the point where I could walk with a single cane.

It's not pretty. As is true for a lot of people with cerebral palsy, my walking is a model of function over form—a halting, jerky gait that has all the fluidity of a car running out of gas. I can't watch video of myself walking. It's not that I'm embarrassed; somehow, in my mind, my movements, while not graceful, don't stand out in a crowd. But seeing myself on video reminds me that I am different, at least in the way I get from one place to another.

Walking also takes a lot more effort for me than it does for most people. The energy I expend walking a mile is equivalent to what you would use running two miles. So walking a thousand miles is like you running from Savannah to San Diego. Plus, I still have to deal with my feet, which aren't perfectly suited for walking. They still curl toward the instep (like someone with a cramp), and my big toe stacks on top of the others. In the beginning of my journey, in order to walk any distance, I had to put numerous bandages on my big toes.

None of that presents a problem when I'm walking a mile. But the average PGA Tour course, when you measure all the distances between holes, is between five and six miles long over some interesting topography. When you walk those distances for four straight days, plus at least one practice round, bandaged toes can get a little sore. By May I had blisters on top of blisters, and by August, the calluses were bulging against the sides of my shoes.

Those were minor annoyances, though, little bothers hardly worth a quibble when you consider I was getting to live out my dream.

Every week, I worked with the tour and picked a player to focus on and interview. Once the player agreed, I followed him during every round, watched him on the range, got to know his caddie and any family members who were out with him, and talked to his fans. Then I spent time with the player, asking questions for my blog on PGATour.com.

What I found interesting were the questions I got asked in return. "How hard is it for you to walk eighteen holes?" was standard, along with, "Do you play golf, and if so, how?" But by far the question I got most was, "How did you decide to do this?"

I always smiled as I answered that one. It was a story in itself.

I've always loved sports. I can barely tear myself away from a good football or basketball game. I even watch badminton during the Olympics. But golf has always been my favorite, in part because of how beautiful and poetic I find the swing when it is executed by a great player, and also because golf was the only sport I could play. Holding myself up on my cane with my left hand, I swing the club one-handed with my right. I play from the forward tees and get around the course without much trouble. I'm not good—far from it—but like millions of amateurs, I don't have to play well to enjoy the game.

Plus, I can play with my dad and mom, the people who have always been there for me, supporting everything I want to achieve. My parents decided early in life that they weren't going to treat me differently from other kids. I went to public school and was expected to do everything the other boys did. If there were places I couldn't go or things I couldn't do, I simply had to adapt. Golf was one of those things.

My father and I had watched golf on television together for as long as I could remember. Once I could get around on a single crutch, I begged him to take me to the golf course. My swing looks more like a tennis player hitting a low forehand ground stroke than anything you might see on tour, but, like everything else, I've learned to adapt. I'll never be a great player, but I have my moments. Like all golfers, I feel a warm satisfaction when I hit a solid shot, and I get a tingle when I feel the buttery soft click of a ball connecting with the sweet spot of a club. I experience the same thrills as any other golfer when a long putt finds the bottom of the hole, and I am just as disgusted with myself when I chunk a shot in the water. I love the smell of freshly mowed greens in the morning and the sounds of irrigation heads clicking to life at dusk. Like a lot of men my age, I am, for lack of a better term, a golf nut.

And I've always been a huge fan of the PGA Tour. When I was twelve years old, Dad took me to my first golf tournament, the Greater Greensboro Open in Greensboro, North Carolina, to see my sporting heroes in the flesh for the first time. Walking the course was still tough for me in those days. Like most twelve-year-olds, I was at an awkward growth stage, which complicated things further for me. Dad and I positioned ourselves near the driving range so I could get autographs as players came out to warm up or came off after finishing their work.

About midmorning, veteran CBS analyst and former U.S. Open winner Ken Venturi saw me and gave me an autograph. He was obviously on his way somewhere—television people don't amble around with nowhere to go—but Ken took the time to speak to Dad and me. Then he did more than sign an autograph. After talking with Dad, Ken put me in the golf cart with him and took me around to get more autographs. He introduced me to players, all of whom took the time to ask questions and talk to me about golf. Then Ken asked if I would like to join him in the television tower behind the eighteenth green.

He didn't have to ask twice. With the help of a couple of volunteers and security personnel, I made it to the best seat on the course.

In the booth beside Ken sat a young Texan, a former college golfer who was in his fifth year working for CBS and seemed to be a rising star. His name was Jim Nantz. I had heard Jim broadcast before, especially during Masters week, but I'd never seen him. While I was intimidated in the beginning (as any twelve-year-old would be), both Jim and Ken went out of their way to make me feel comfortable.

From there, two lasting friendships ensued. Dad took me back to Greensboro every year, and every year Ken and Jim would invite me into the booth. I became a regular part of the telecast and great friends with two of the nicest men in the world. There are a lot of egos in television. As I've gotten older I've come to understand what Hunter S. Thompson meant when he said, "The TV business is uglier than most things. It is normally perceived as some kind of cruel and shallow money trench through the heart of the journalism industry, a long plastic hallway where thieves and pimps run free and good men die like dogs, for no good reason." Ken Venturi and Jim Nantz are the exceptions. Television would be a shining example of all things good if everyone in the business were like Ken and Jim.

I kept in touch with Ken after he retired to his home in California, and I make it a point to see him whenever I travel to the West Coast. Jim and I have become great friends. It was he who said, "I've got an idea," as we were talking about how to make my dream of following the tour a reality.

"I know you want to follow the tour and write a book, which is a great idea, so why don't you write up a proposal for [PGA Tour commissioner] Tim Finchem," Jim said. "Outline what you want to do and how you'll go about doing it."

"Be happy to, Jim," I said, "but I'm sure Tim has better things to do than read a letter from me. I'm sure he has his mail screened. By the time he gets it, if he gets it at all, the season'll be half over."

"No," Jim said, "you're not going to send it to him. You're going to give it to me, and I'm going to hand-deliver it to Tim and tell him this is something the tour needs to do."

Jim was emphatic, so I did what he suggested: I wrote up the idea of walking every round of every event, interviewing players, and writing about it on the tour's Web site. Good to his word, Jim delivered the proposal to Tim Finchem and made a persuasive pitch. I've seen Jim do this kind of thing before. He has a hypnotic power of persuasion. His roommates at the University of Houston (one of whom was Masters winner Fred Couples) always said that if he didn't make it in television he could always run for president. By the time Jim finished, Commissioner Finchem probably would have bought whatever he was selling. Thankfully, he was selling me.

So, because of the random kindness of Ken Venturi, and the generous friendship of Jim Nantz, I was given the opportunity to live out the dream of a lifetime. For forty-six weeks I would travel with the

PGA Tour and chronicle my experiences. I couldn't wait. I told my friends that, yeah, it was a tough duty, I would have to work weekends, but, hey, a man's got to do what he has to do.

But for all of my bravado and as thrilled as I was about the prospects of this incredible journey— especially with all the fascinating people I was sure to meet along the way—I was a little anxious about walking twenty to thirty miles a week for the better part of a year, especially along some of the terrain I'd seen on television.

Those concerns sailed away in the breezy thoughts of the year I was about to have. This was going to be the most spectacular season anybody would ever spend. I had to bite my lip when I told people about it. "Yeah," I said with as straight a face as I could muster, "I'll be working."

CHAPTER TWO

Boo Knows Golf

For most people, Maui can elicit a lot of feelings: excitement, peace, happiness, relaxation, and romance, among others. My overwhelming emotion was anxiety.

If I had to start my quest somewhere, Hawaii in January was as good a place as any. The Mercedes-Benz Championship has been played at Kapalua on the island of Maui since 1999. Prior to that, the event was in California. It's one of the longest-running events on tour, going back to 1953 when Al Besselink won the first Tournament of Champions at the Desert Inn Golf Club in Las Vegas. Every year since

17

then, the tour has rewarded winners from the previous year with a tournament all their own. Now the reward is doubled—players get to take their families to Maui in the middle of the winter.

This begs the question: Why was I so anxious? Well, in addition to the butterflies that go with starting any new endeavor, I was shocked when I saw the golf course. As breathtaking as the island is, the Plantation Course at Kapalua is one of the hilliest I've ever seen. It isn't quite as steep as the Road to Hana, but it's not exactly the flat plains of Kansas, either. Maui is perhaps the only island in America where you can go surfing and get a little sun on the beach in the morning, drive several miles up a winding road, and have a snowball fight. It is an island of exquisite beauty and dramatic extremes, a fantastic place to spend your honeymoon but a tough spot to start my yearlong walkabout.

Ben Crenshaw and his partner Bill Coore did a great job building the Plantation Course, especially given the ruggedness of the topography. Ben has long been known as a design "minimalist," which means he moves very little earth and lets the lay of the land dictate the routing. When the land is the side of a mountain, that can be tough, but even so, the Plantation Course is one of the best on tour. Players love it, even though some of the distances between holes are extreme. Walking off the fifth green, for example, you are a mile away from the sixth tee. Players are shuttled between those holes, but the ride takes upward of five minutes, just long enough for your muscles to cool down and stiffen.

Tour officials were kind enough to let me ride on those sorts of interludes. On holes like the eighteenth, however, I was on my own. The par-5 finishing hole is 663 yards long, the longest hole on tour and the longest on the course by a wide margin. It is also straight downhill, dropping more than two hundred feet from tee to green.

People who write travel reviews have said that the view from the eighteenth tee is one of the most breathtaking on all the islands of Hawaii. My breath was taken away, but for a different reason. Walking downhill is much harder for me than walking up-hill because of the way I have to tilt myself. Head-ing downhill, I have to position my weight forward for balance. Although I've never done it, people tell me this is like downhill skiing where you have to lean down the hill to keep from plowing your bottom through the snow. Just as skiers have some spectacu-lar end-over-end tumbles, I've taken my share of falls walking downhill, especially when momentum car-ries me faster than I can move my cane.

Falling is a part of life for me. Throughout my childhood and even as a young adult, I can't remem-ber a time when I didn't have scraped, scabbed, bruised, or otherwise red and sore knees from the in-evitable spills I deal with regularly. Through years of practice I've become an expert at breaking my falls, but that doesn't mean I'm in control. If I were, I wouldn't fall in the first place. When you've adapted your feet, legs, and hips to work in a way other than how the Good Lord designed them, you have to live with a certain level of instability.

One of my most spectacular tumbles came when I was in college in Massachusetts. A friend and I were on our way back home after class when my cane broke. The pieces of the cane went one way and I went the other, which wouldn't have been so bad, except that I blocked traffic on a busy street in both directions for several minutes while my friend came back to help me up.

Because walking is such a big deal for me, I kept a journal of the number of steps I took and the number of times I fell during my time on tour. I felt as though people would be interested in knowing how many steps it took me to get around a golf course (about double the amount of the average person) and how many spills I took along the way. A great day, especially since I'm in my thirties and not as buoyant as I used to be, was one when I got to write 0 in the fall column.

Thankfully I didn't do any headers down the hills at Kapalua. It turned out to be a great week, in part because I realized that if I could get around a course that severe, I could probably get around any course on tour. Not to be cute, but it was all downhill from there. It was also a fantastic week, because I got to spend it with golf's newest everyman superstar: Milton, Florida's finest, Boo Weekley.

You know you're in for a treat when the guy you're spending the week with is named after the cartoon sidekick on the old *Yogi Bear* show. To some the moniker "good ole boy," which was coined by Tom Wolfe in 1965 in a piece about NASCAR driver Junior Johnson called "The Last American Hero," has become a politically incorrect put-down, a pejorative to be avoided. Boo loves it. "Heck, yeah, you can call me a good ole boy," he has said on numerous occasions. "I hope that's what I am. Beats the heck out of not being one."

When I first met Thomas Brent "Boo" Weekley, he was eight months away from being the hero of the Ryder Cup. He was famous, however, as the guy who wore camouflage dri-FITs at the British Open and told the BBC that he had no idea St. Andrews was the home of golf—"I thought my hometown of Milton, Florida, was," he said with an innocent smile. Then, of Scottish food, he said, "It's different eatin' here than back home. Ain't got no sweet tea, and ain't got no fried chicken."

To call Boo unpretentious doesn't do him justice. A good ole boy who grew up raising cows on his grandparents' place in Milton, an on-the-way-to-nowhere town between Alabama and the Gulf of Mexico, Boo used to wrangle alligators off of his porch and back to the swamp when the Blackwater River flooded and deposited the critters at his doorstep. He went to Abraham Baldwin Agricultural College in Tifton, Georgia, where he played golf in rain pants because cotton twill made him itch. Now he is one of the most beloved champions on the PGA Tour. He dips Skoal, lived in a double-wide trailer while his house was being built, even after winning his first tour event— "It was a pretty nice double-wide. I've been in a whole lot worse"—he has Mossy Oak and Bass Pro Shops as sponsors, and the week I met him, he'd been detained by the TSA at the airport when he failed to unpack a couple of thirty-caliber bullets after returning from a hunting trip.

"It was just one them thangs," Boo said with a wink and a shrug.

I wasn't sure if he knew what to expect when we met. This being the first event of the season, people on tour had heard about what I was doing, but nobody had actually seen me. I've gotten used to the stares over the years. It happens all the time, usually with kids, so when it's appropriate I take time to explain what cerebral palsy is and what it isn't. For centuries, people with cerebral palsy were locked in mental institutions. Among the many blessings I've experienced are the teachable moments my situation has provided, especially to children. Of course, I figured Boo had been around people with cerebral palsy before, but I still wasn't sure how he would react.

He did better than most adults I meet. When you've been the object of stares your whole life you understand what's happening when men look at you and instantly find something fascinating on the pavement or in the trees. Boo checked me out the way he would a pro-am partner, "sizin' me up," he called it. Then we shook hands and went about our week like old friends.

None of what the public sees from Boo Weekley is an act. He is the affable country boy, a guy who knows more about trotlines than tea parties, a guy who couldn't pick Queen Elizabeth out of a lineup but who would call her ma'am anyway, because ma'am and sir is what you do. Boo is the guy in the background when the bust goes down on *Cops*, the one in flip-flops and a T-shirt with his arms folded across his ample belly. He is everyman. He is us.

We talked about the possibility of his making the Ryder Cup team, an eventuality that would propel him onto the world stage in ways he could never have imagined. "Well, I'd like to play, but, you know, if I don't, it ain't gonna hurt my feelin's. I just want to play the game of golf, play it as long as I can, get out when I can still enjoy my life, enjoy my son and be able to show him things that my daddy got to show me. You know, that's what it's about for me—family. I like to be fishin' and huntin', you know, and they're right there with me when I'm doing it. I miss the opportunity to be able to do that."

Not only did he eventually make the Ryder Cup team, he went on to become the hero and emotional leader of the American squad. Where past U.S. Ryder Cup team captains had relied on cheerleaders from players' alma maters, or tear-jerking videos, or profound readings or speeches from past, present, and future presidents, Paul Azinger relied on Boo to tell stories about alligator wrestling and climbing into the boxing ring with an orangutan only to get knocked out cold in fifteen seconds.

Boo would become famous for making up the word "compatibate," a hybrid of "compatible" and "motivate," which was at once hilarious and right on point. On Sunday, after hitting his opening tee shot, he straddled his driver like a hobbyhorse and gal-loped down the fairway slapping the grip like a quarter horse. The crowd loved it. And they loved him. Boo won two matches, lost none, and tied one, but his influence was far greater than the scoreboard. By the end of the week, the galleries were chanting, "Boo-S-A! Boo-S-A!"

I was thrilled that America got to meet the man I became friends with the first week of the season.

This week Boo's wife, Karyn, and son, Parker, traveled with him to Hawaii along with his mother, Patsy. Maui is family week. The tour calls it a "limited field" event, meaning that it isn't open to all players. Davis Love used to call it "the ultimate incentive to win one, because the wife and kids love going to Maui." Boo had won for the first time at the previous year's Verizon Heritage on Hilton Head.

"Where do you eat on the road?" I asked. Boo is a big guy who hasn't missed many meals. He is the first to tell you how much he enjoys a good meal and a frosty beverage after a round.

"We'll go to Burger King or McDonald's or Chick-fil-A," he said. "Maybe ever' now and then

I'll splurge a little bit and get some fancy food at Outback or Carrabba's or stuff like 'at. If it was up to me, we'd rent a house ever' week and have cereal for breakfast, ham sandwiches, bananas, sardines, whatever we want to eat. I mean, I ain't gotta have all that; I know what it takes to survive."

Parker didn't take well to Hawaii. He loved the ocean, but the views didn't hold the attention of a first grader for very long. He was ready to head home by the weekend. "Spoiled son, that's what you are," Boo said. "You ain't nothing but spoiled."

"How did you get into the game?" I asked.

"Well, I played all of the sports I could play, and I had an accident in about ever' other sport. I either broke my fangers, broke my shoulder, tore up my shoulder, tore up my knees, messed up my ankles. I thought I might get into somethin' wasn't such a contact sport.

"Then I happened to be out with some friends when we was in the eighth grade and the high school golf coach was with the golf team. They was a coupla holes over from us, but they kinda run side by side. So I hit a ball, and pulled-hooked it, and hit the golf coach. Well, it was just rolling and it hit him in the ankle. Course, you ever hit yourself in the ankle, you know it hurts.

"He went to hollerin' and I walked over there. Him and my daddy knew each other 'cause they deer hunted together. So I was apologizing, and he looked at me and said, 'You're a Weekley.' I said, 'Yes, sir.' And he said, 'What are you doing playing golf?' I said, 'I'm trying something new,' and he said, 'I'll talk to you later.'

"I figured I'd never hear from the man again. Next thing I know here we are about a month and a half later, two months, maybe, and he's wanting to teach me how to play golf. We went from there. He flipped me from left-handed to right-handed. I'd played baseball and everything left-handed but batted both ways, so it was easy to switch over.

"That's how I got started. Ever' mornin' in the summertime he'd pick me up and teach me how to play."

Boo didn't have the greatest week on the golf course in Maui, although he appeared to enjoy the sights and sounds of the island. He even got a kick out of the opening ceremonies, where virtuoso Jake Shimabukuro played the National Anthem on the ukulele. Now, that was something you don't see every day!

"What'd you do with the family this week?" I asked.

"We ain't done much," he said. "We went down to Lululala."

It took a second for me to realize what he was trying to say. "You mean Lahaina?" I asked.

He laughed. "I can't pronounce that. Yeah, we went down there and walked around. They got this tree down there, dude, it's unreal! It's like just one stump, but the tree covers a circle 'bout seventy or eighty yards. It's got roots that come out of the tree and then go down in the ground and come back up, sorta like a Spanish oak back home. Man, it's just funny-looking, but it's a big ol' tree, dude. I bet that trunk's prob'ly ever' bit of ten yards wide. Other than that, we ain't done nothing; we just been at the house hanging out. With the rain, it's kind of hard to get out and about with my little boy."

Dad and I saw a little bit of Maui while we were there, thanks in no small part to Tom Vavra, our driver for the week. The resort provided courtesy ground transportation, and Tom did a wonderful job of getting us from the golf course to the hotel. Not only that, he sent me weekly e-mails of encouragement for the rest of the year. Many times during those waning summer months, when my feet hurt or I'd battled travel nightmares, Tom's messages provided the pick-me-up I needed to keep going—another random act from a passing acquaintance that elevated my spirits and made me realize that what I was doing really meant something to others.

Boo shot 80 on opening day. This sent my anxiety level through the roof. The last thing I wanted to do was intrude on a player who had given up the baseball pitcher equivalent of an eight-run first inning. "What do I do now?" I asked my dad, who was standing beside me near the scoring trailer.

"Just hang around and see what happens," Dad said.

A few minutes later, Boo came out and found me. "Wow, thanks for coming," I said.

He smiled and said, "I told you I'd be here."

"I know, but you didn't play well, so . . ."

"Listen, golf's just a game. It ain't life or death. If I tell you I'm gonna do somethin', I'm gonna do it."

Boo's golf got better every day after that. He shot 74 on Friday and finished the weekend with rounds of 68 and 66.

Saturday, he played in just over three hours, which made it tough to keep up. After a couple of rounds, walking a course becomes easier, because I have a route mapped out. I know which spots are difficult and where I can walk to minimize the prospects of slipping and falling. What makes a place like Maui tough is how quickly the weather can change. A rain burst can (and often does) come out of nowhere and drench the course for five minutes; then the sun reappears just as quickly. For most people this is a minor annoyance—getting your shorts wet or muffing a hairdo—but wet conditions require me to change the way I walk. So much of my balance depends on my ability to lead with my cane and lean my weight into the step that traction is a big concern. Morning dew or a flash shower can completely alter my approach. Not only did Boo play early and fast on Saturday, but we'd also had rain, which made for dicey conditions.

I managed okay; better, in fact, than Boo's mother. Because I know the hazards of wet conditions, I always pay attention to the ground situation. Patsy Weekley was not quite as aware. On the eighth tee, she hit a slick spot and went flying. Spinning tires at a tractor pull couldn't have thrown more mud skyward. Patsy let out a whoop as she went down in a perfect split beside the gallery ropes.

Boo made sure we got a photo. The Boo Crew wanted that one on the wall of the new house, "or the trailer if we don't ever get it done."

As we were saying our good-byes on Sunday to the sound of ukuleles with a giant orange sun dipping below the waterline on the horizon, Boo said, "Hey, how many times did you fall this week?"

"None," I said.

He grinned and pointed to Patsy. "Mamma's already one up on you."

CHAPTER THREE

FIRST SLIP

My second week in Hawaii couldn't have been more different from the first. For starters, the Sony Open is the first full-field event of the year, so instead of 31 players as we had in the Mercedes-Benz Championship, the Sony started with 144. The tour also moved from Maui to Honolulu, which is like moving from Aspen to Cleveland. All of Hawaii is paradise, but some parts are more bejeweled than others. Honolulu is like any capital city: tough and commercial, even the beaches. Plus, it's flat. Where the Plantation Course at Kapalua is one of the hilliest and toughest courses in the world to walk, Waialae

Country Club, home of the Sony Open, is one of the easiest to navigate, with very few elevation changes and many parallel fairways. Which makes my two falls all the more ironic.

Waialae reminded me a lot of Greensboro Country Club in North Carolina, where I first started thinking of myself as a golfer. I'm the youngest of three children. Both my parents are avid golfers. From the beginning it was the family activity, so when we kids got old enough to play, it was our activity as well. My brother didn't play, but my sister, four and a half years older, was accomplished enough to play competitive college golf. Even at thirteen she was showing the kind of promise that would make her a four-year starter on her high school men's golf team. I was nine when Mom and Dad had me join the family on the course. Since I swung with one arm and lacked the ability to use my lower body in the swing, my distance suffered. I teed off from the 150-yard marker on par 4s and then moved back to the 200-yard mark on par 5s. My sister insisted that

I play from the forward tees on the par 3s, which was fine with me. It took about three holes during our first round for the two of us to start competing with each other.

Those memories flooded back like a warm sea spray as I walked onto Waialae Country Club. I could almost see my family playing this course, my sister and me ragging on each other as we tried to beat each other's brains out.

This was reinforced when I met my player for the week, Brandt Snedeker, two years removed from being an All-American at Vanderbilt, and the PGA Tour rookie of the year. "The thing I remember most about growing up is just playing golf with my dad and brother on the weekends," Brandt said. "It's kind of the thing we did together. We would go out every Saturday or Sunday and play nine or eighteen holes. It's the way we spent time together. I can remember trying to beat my brother, trying to beat my dad; I kind of got the competitive juices going, not wanting to lose to anybody. You know how that goes."

I did indeed know how it went.

"My grandmother gave me my first set of clubs when I was six," he continued. "I played everything growing up: golf, baseball, basketball, you name it, I played it. I realized that I was better at golf than everything else, so I just stuck with that. Things kind of blossomed from there."

Brandt was still getting his sea legs after a whirlwind rookie year. He came out like a wide-eyed kid and made his mark early. In the Buick Invitational at Torrey Pines, he shot 61 on the North Course, a score that was achingly close to golf's gold standard of 59, a score that has still been posted only three times in the history of the PGA Tour, and never by a rookie. (For those of you keeping track, the 59ers were Al Geiberger in 1977, Chip Beck in 1991, and David Duval in 1999.)

"It was surreal," he said. "I remember I looked around on the tenth hole and I had like ten thousand people following me. It was my third tournament of the year. Nobody knew who I was or what I was doing. I didn't really know what I was doing, to be honest. My hand was shaking so bad. I said, 'Oh my God, I'm ten under after ten. If you're ever going to shoot fifty-nine now's the time. It's not going to get any easier. Just birdie three holes coming in.' But I wasn't able to do it. It was still a great experience, especially to get in that position early in the year in San Diego with Tiger being there. Being around that kind of media atmosphere, being around that kind of competition for the first time, it was instrumental in my development."

Brandt won the Wyndham Championship in my hometown of Greensboro, North Carolina, at Forest Oaks, one of the oldest courses to host a tour event. "That was a great memory, obviously," he said.

Being named rookie of the year was a great memory as well. "Something I wasn't expecting," he said. "It's very humbling to have your peers out here vote for you and give you a reward like that. But now the pressure's on, you know. Now that everybody thinks I'm pretty good, I've got to follow up and prove them all right."

Unfortunately, it wouldn't be this week.

I think the bad luck started during Wednesday's pro-am round. While Tuesday and Wednesday are technically practice round days, Wednesdays are for entertainment. Aside from title sponsorship and television revenue, the primary source of cash flow for individual tournaments is the pro-am, where amateur golfers of all makes and models pay between $2,000 and $6,000 to play with a pro. That's what makes golf unique among professional sports. No one who buys a ticket to an NFL game expects to go out for a pass in the warm-ups, or kick a few field goals at halftime. No tennis fan expects to warm up against Rafael Nadal before a tournament. But almost every week, several hundred golf fans get to play the tournament course the day before the event begins, with a tour pro. Brandt and his group did fine in the pro-am, but I set the tone for the week when I had my first fall.

It seemed silly. The course was as flat as West Texas and as dry as the last meal I tried to cook. Then, out of the blue as I walked toward the media center, my cane slipped and I went down.

"You okay?" someone asked.

I draw attention when I fall. People watch me, even if they go to great pains to appear as though they're looking elsewhere. Whenever I take a spill I always hear some hoots and a gasp or two. Good Samaritans have a way of materializing out of nowhere when a young man with cerebral palsy takes a tumble. This was no exception. It was no big deal. I was up and walking again in no time. But once again, for a few brief moments, I was the center of unwanted attention. No matter how often it happens, that's still a hard pill to swallow.

Thankfully, it didn't happen during the tournament or as I was following Brandt. He finished his pro-am round and seemed upbeat as we talked about our shared love of college football and fishing. "I love sport fishing and I do a lot of ocean fishing," he said. "I go down to the Keys a lot. Then when we get back in we do normal stuff at home. We spend so little time at home that when we're there we see movies and catch up on normal stuff. I love watching college football, even Vanderbilt. We're getting better every year. Not the doormat of the SEC anymore."

I asked him if he had any superstitions. It wasn't an off-the-wall question. Throughout the years, I'd noticed a lot of players develop idiosyncrasies that bordered on voodoo. Some players will use only broken tees on par 3s, because they once had a hole in one with a broken tee. Others wear a specific color on a particular day because their career-low round came while wearing that particular hue.

"It's weird. When you start playing good, you think it's what you had to eat or something," he said. "At San Diego last year when I played good, I didn't have dinner the night before I went out and played, so I always made sure I ate a late lunch and didn't eat dinner all week. I remember on the Nationwide Tour we had Dairy Queen every night one week that I won. You think it's the most random stuff, but you don't want to switch it up. So, yeah, I have superstitions. I always mark my ball with a quarter from the sixties that's heads up. Besides that, I always wear blue on

Sunday. I don't know why. I just kind of like wearing blue."

The other party in Brandt's "we" was his fiancée (now his wife), Mandy Tothe, who followed him every step in Honolulu. She couldn't have been kinder. When I asked her what she enjoyed most about being on tour, I expected something like "exotic locations" or "how pampered we are by the tournament officials." Instead, Mandy said she liked "being able to see Brandt on a daily basis instead of once every three weeks."

It was good to see that she had the right attitude for a tour wife before they were married.

Despite the love and support of a good woman, and the diligent presence of his shadow for the week (me), Brandt had a rough couple of days. He shot 2 under par on Thursday, but shot 2 over on Friday, a round that included a trip into a muck pit. After hitting his tee shot right into a hazard on the ninth hole, Brandt rolled up his trouser leg and waded into the black primordial goo to hit his ball out. Afterward he said, "I hit it right into some sludge, and it was about calf deep, but I was able to get a club on it. I stunk the rest of the day. I think there was some sewage in there, but I was able to save a shot."

Whether or not it was an ominous sign, I fell again on Friday. And again I attracted a crowd. Thankfully, I was up in no time, and the ruckus didn't seem to disturb Brandt.

He had more important and, it would turn out, more controversial things to worry about. When the second round was over, it appeared as though Brandt would play the weekend. The cut line was even par. According to the rules as everyone understood them, the low seventy players and ties after thirty-six holes made the cut and played the weekend. When the final putt fell on Friday, eighteen players were tied for seventieth place at even par. Among them was Brandt Snedeker.

Then the tour implemented its newest and, as it would turn out, most short-lived rule, saying that if the cut exceeded seventy-eight players, the number closest to seventy would play the weekend. In this case, that number was sixty-nine players at 1 under or better. The other eighteen were credited with having made the cut, given last-place money, and sent on their way.

"I don't know anything about it," Brandt said. "I just found out about it. I was all excited because I thought I made the cut, and now they tell me they got a new cut rule this year and if there's more than seventy-eight guys, they go to the next number down. So I have the weekend off."

The rule didn't survive the first blossoms of spring. After an outcry from a majority of players, most of whom detested the "squishiness" of the new system, the old cut rule was reinstituted, and life went back to normal on tour. That didn't help Brandt Snedeker in Hawaii, but he didn't seem terribly upset. After all, he and Mandy had the weekend together in paradise.

I had no such luxury. Brandt missing the cut didn't let me off the hook. I still had two rounds to walk. So I chose one of the most popular players on tour to follow: Fred Funk.

A former college golf coach, the fifty-year-old Funk is the epitome of the happy golfer. There is nothing prima donna–like about Fred or his wife, Sharon. Walking with Sharon and listening to Fred interact with the gallery, I quickly shed my role as a diarist and slipped on the comfortable slippers of fandom. But as we made the turn on Sunday afternoon, my role in this odyssey was brought back to me when a stranger walked up with his hand outstretched.

"D.J., my name is Robert Havrilak," he said. Robert was a large fellow who walked with a limp. "I saw you on the Golf Channel," he continued. "Quite a story. I said to myself, 'You know, if that man can walk every round of golf on tour this year, the least I can do is go out to the tour event right down the street and walk the final round.' So here I am. You inspired me to be here. Good luck to you."

From that moment forward, I never took a day of my journey for granted.

CHAPTER FOUR

"LEAVE THE WORLD BETTER THAN YOU FOUND IT"

I didn't start out to inspire anyone. My dream was to follow golf, to be out on the most beautiful courses, walking with the greatest players in the world. At first, I considered writing a travel column or maybe assembling a "how to follow the PGA Tour" book that would include things like where to eat in Fort Worth during the Crowne Plaza Invitational at Colonial or where to stay in Moline, Illinois, if you're there for the John Deere Classic. I also knew I could tell stories that people don't get through traditional media. I had no intention of asking players about what they just shot or what tournament they were playing next. I intended to ask things like, "Who inspired you most growing up?" or "When did you start to believe you could make a living as a professional athlete and what event pushed you toward golf?" As a fan, those were the questions I wanted answered, so those were the ones I hoped to ask.

Hoping for it wasn't going to get me very far, so I decided to conduct a little experiment. I'd met Aaron Baddeley back in 2003 at the Arnold Palmer Invitational Presented by MasterCard. He was play-ing with Jeff Sluman, whom I've known since I was in high school. I didn't stalk Aaron or anything, but being part of the gallery, I struck up a conversation with his fiancée (now his wife), Richelle. Afterward, I met Aaron and we all exchanged e-mail addresses. A few years later, when I realized I was going back to Bay Hill, I contacted Aaron and asked, "How would you like to be the test subject for a little project I'm working on?"

He jumped at the idea. "You know, I have a lot of friends who want to know what it's like to travel on tour," he said. "This sounds like the perfect way to tell them." So I walked with Aaron in Orlando, and we spent time together after his rounds. Then I wrote up my original proposal and showed it to Jim Nantz.

"Everything you have in here's great," Jim said. "But I'm not interested in your restaurant recommendations. I want to know what it's like for you to walk around a golf course. I want to know why you love golf so much that you'd walk a thousand miles to watch it. That, and your interaction with the players, is what will make this thing fly."

I was thrilled by Jim's reaction, but I wasn't convinced. "Why would anyone want to read about me walking?" I asked.

Jim cocked his head and said, "Deej, this might come as a shock to you, but you have cerebral palsy."

"Shhh, don't tell anybody."

"Seriously, that's the story people want to read. It'll inspire them."

That was great to hear, but I still wasn't sure. Later, once my yearlong odyssey was complete and I could reflect on the experience through the lens of hindsight, I realized that my story, for whatever reason, did inspire people. Every week someone would come up to me and say, "I heard about what you're doing, and it's really motivated me to get out and chase my dreams." Those were the most satisfying words I'd ever heard, even though at first I didn't understand why I was special.

Later, I realized that my story touched a collective nerve, because I am different: not different in the sense that I'm disabled, but different because I have never once thought of myself as having a disability. I've certainly never played the victim card or felt the need to wave my arms and shout, "Look at me, I'm overcoming obstacles." I have always surrounded myself with people who couldn't care less that I have cerebral palsy. When my friends have said things

like, "Hey, Deej, let's go shoot hoops" or "Deej, you
want to go play golf?" I always figured out a way to
be involved. Sometimes, like in basketball, the games
had to be modified, but that was no big deal. I looked
at it like having a handicap in golf. I just had to invent
games that leveled the playing field so I could partici-
pate.

A lot of people say they don't want to be looked at
as being disabled, but many of them don't mind the
special treatment or the sympathy or the perks. I have
no patience for those people. I never will.

Jim Nantz saw that trait in me before I recognized
it in myself. He also understood the power of the
book you now hold. "Just think of the one guy who
might find the strength to go out and try something
new or work toward a goal because of your story,"
Jim said. "If you can do it, I think this would be one
of the greatest stories of the year."

"Oh, I can do it," I said.

"Have you ever walked four rounds of a golf
tournament?"

"Sure, just not for forty-six weeks. But I'm sure it won't be a problem."

He smiled and shook his head.

This wasn't puffery or an inflated ego; it was just the mind-set I brought to every challenge. My parents gave me a lot, but one of the most important traits I inherited was a stubborn streak, one that served me well as I fought the inevitable battles of life, and one that would carry me through the tough days I was bound to have on tour. As easy as I made the whole thing sound when talking to Jim, deep down I knew that walking a thousand miles was a daunting task. Thankfully, I had always heard the words "you won't be able to do that" as a challenge. Quiet determination had been bred into me. When the doctors told Mom and Dad, "He'll never walk," they didn't accept it. They found surgeons who would cut my adductor muscles, straighten my legs, and at least give me a fighting chance at mobility. When I was told I would need to attend a school away from my friends and siblings because of handicap accessibility, I said no, thank you, and figured out a way to navigate the staircases and hallways of my local public school. Sometimes it took a little imagination—I needed to go down stairs backward, dragging my cane like a ski pole—and sometimes it took me a little longer to do things, but I always found a way. Adapting becomes instinctual when nothing fits your needs, and pushing yourself to the limit becomes as natural as breathing. If it's the only way to move forward and experience the normal pleasures of life, you become creative. And you become driven.

Even after Jim convinced Commissioner Tim Finchem that my story was worthwhile, I still had to convince some skeptics at the tour. First, the media staff wanted to see how I would handle following a player for a week. Sportswriters who cover golf are given special access in return for certain responsibilities. For example, writers and photographers can get credentials allowing them to walk on the players' side of the gallery ropes along with the caddies, walking scorers, and marshals. As long as they stay

out of the way and kneel or sit during shots so as not
to obstruct the views of paying customers, journalists get an unobstructed view of the action. Just how
I would do walking inside the ropes was a question
even I couldn't answer. I certainly wouldn't blend in,
and the last thing tour officials needed was someone
distracting the players.

Then there was the time I would need with the
athletes. Tour officials were concerned about impos-
ing on their players. A lot of people say, "Hey, how
tough can it be? These guys play golf for a living."
But tour players have obligations that extend far beyond showing up for their tee times and signing their
scorecards. Thousands of fans want autographs,
sponsors want them to glad-hand with VIPs, friends
want tickets, agents want a few minutes to talk about
the latest shirt deals, and local television and news-
paper reporters want quotes for their stories. Players also have to make their own travel, lodging, and
eating arrangements, in addition to carving out time
to practice. Just how I was going to blend into that

demanding stew was a question tour officials needed to answer before signing on to my idea.

They liked the fact that I had already done a test run with Aaron, so officials decided to repeat my example and run a two-week experiment. They would have me follow players for two consecutive weeks to gauge my fatigue and see how players reacted to me.

I think the results surprised them. Not only did I walk every step of the Barclays and the Deutsche Bank Championship without complaint, but I didn't disrupt anyone, and players seemed genuinely pleased to have me around. For starters, I didn't intrude. The inside-the-ropes credential was nice, but I used it as infrequently as possible. When the crowds overwhelmed, I would slip inside the gallery ropes for a few holes, but I stayed well behind everyone. The last thing I wanted was for some player to see me and say, "What's up with that guy?" Then during the interviews, I let my players know that I was writing from a fan's perspective; I wasn't there to talk about their rounds or to ask any probing or uncomfortable questions. I approached the job as a fan and asked things that fans wanted to know. Everyone appreciated my candor and even thanked me for being out there.

Player reactions (along with the fact that I didn't tumble down a hill and somersault across a green during any pivotal competitive moments) convinced tour officials that I had a viable plan. Having me out there every week would give local reporters another early human-interest story, and my columns on PGATour.com would give fans an insider's look at what it's like on tour week in and week out.

Of course, I was on my own when it came to travel. The tour provided me with media credentials and they coordinated the interviews, but just like the players I was an independent contractor responsible for my own expenses.

"Great job you got there, D.J.," my dad said. "Now, how are you going to pay to travel around the country for forty-four weeks?"

I had no idea. Thankfully, my friends came through again. Through various contacts, I got an audience with Whitney Eichinger, the marketing director for Southwest Airlines. Once I explained what I would be doing, Whitney said, "Just tell me what you need."

Southwest became my first in-kind sponsor, providing me with something called "must ride" passes, a priority nonrevenue seat on any flight, the kind of ticket used by flight attendants who live and work in different cities.

With that sponsorship in hand, my next call was to Marriott. After a similar pitch, the Marriott golf marketing director said the company would love to put me up in Marriott properties. And that's how it started. Armed with two in-kind sponsorships to soften the financial blow of travel costs, I set out for a year on tour. The fact that I had no real idea what I was doing didn't bother me at all. Several months later, Accusplit approached me with an offer to wear their pedometer for the rest of the year. Ashworth then offered me a clothing deal, and FootJoy came forward to provide me with shoes. Before long Outback Steakhouse asked if I'd like gift certificates to eat at their restaurants, and Canon provided me with a camera. It happened slowly, but by the end of the year players were giving me grief about looking like a NASCAR driver because of all the sponsor logos on my shirts.

I ribbed them right back. Friends needle friends. It's part of the game of golf.

Things weren't quite as comfortable in the third week of the season when the tour arrived in California. Not only did I know very few players at that point, I was still feeling my way through the nuances of tour life. What I know now that I didn't fully understand at the time is that the tour is, for lack of a better analogy, a well-heeled traveling circus. The towns and courses are different every week, but the core group, the performers, support staff, national journalists, and television people, are the same: a relatively small cadre of gypsies bound together by a life on the road.

Comfort is often found in the consistent rhythms that permeate every event. All the locker rooms from

Maui to Miami to Milwaukee have sitting areas where players can make phone calls, meet with their agents, or just relax before or after a round. Player dining is always private and isolated, although it can be anything but quiet, especially in the summer when wives and children travel with their husbands. The media tent (and it is almost always a nice tent) is near the eighteenth green, the driving range, putting green, parking lot, clubhouse, or some combination thereof. The grandstands are always curtained with thick green tarps, the caddie pens are always within spitting distance of the cart barns, the volunteers are smartly dressed and well trained, and the range balls are shiny and new. Reps from every golf company under the sun mill around the locker rooms and driving ranges like street-corner hustlers, and refrigerator-size boxes full of clubs, bags, balls, and clothing pour into each site, taking up every vacant corner until claimed by the players. Trailers outfitted with shafts, grips, buffing wheels, and all the necessary paraphernalia to create a golf club out of component parts line the ranges, and mobile television compounds are squirreled away behind bushes or in some other "nonessential" area.

Tour regulars become like family. Tournament directors and rules officials, people like Slugger White, Mark Russell, and Mike Shea, whom no one outside of golf has ever heard of, greet you like a relative at a train station each week, and every player has someone from the tour's travel staff on speed dial.

Joel Schuchmann, the senior manager of communications, a soft-spoken guy about my age who spent several years with the American Junior Golf Association before joining the tour, was one of the people who helped me each week, along with Doug Milne, a gregarious communications manager who went to great lengths to make sure everybody was happy. Media officials like John Bush, Joe Chemycz, Joan Alexander, and Stewart Moore were there for me as well. Seeing them each week made me feel like I was home even when we were in a city I'd never visited.

Such was the case with Palm Springs, where Joan

and John helped arrange for me to follow Shaun Micheel, winner of the 2003 PGA Championship.

I'd never been to Palm Springs, so seeing this golf oasis in the high desert of California was a treat, especially in January. The Sinatra compound is on the main road through town. A mile farther out is the Annenberg estate, where President Reagan used to play golf every New Year's Day. It's a beautiful place to spend the winter. That's why in the early months of the season the tour conducts what it calls its West Coast swing, a series of tournaments in Hawaii, California, and Arizona, where the weather is warm and the time zones are such that televised golf doesn't conflict with the NFL playoffs. The first event on the mainland is the Bob Hope Chrysler Classic, the last of the celebrity-titled tournaments, contested within sight of Bob's Palm Springs home. Back in the sixties and seventies, every celebrity worth his salt had a tournament named after him. Bing Crosby, Danny Thomas, Jackie Gleason, Sammy Davis Jr., and even the Rhinestone Cowboy, Glen Campbell, had a tournament.

Today, all that's left is the Hope, a special event in a special place honoring one of the all-time great entertainers. For years the California crowd came out in droves for the Hope, a pro-am that featured a who's who of movie stars and entertainers. Everybody from Randolph Scott to Evel Knievel to President Gerald Ford played. When Bob called, you came. Since Hope's death, the tournament has been hosted by George Lopez, but for the foreseeable future Arnold Palmer, a great friend of Hope's, will be the honorary master of ceremonies.

It remains a pro-am, and a unique event of the season since it is played over five days (ninety holes instead of seventy-two) on four different courses. This was a challenge for me, because I like familiarity. Walking a different course each day forced me to keep an eye out for any perilous holes or slick spots. I fell twice in thirty seconds at the Hope, tripping over the same television cable like Curly in a Three Stooges skit. Dad got a kick out of that.

Thankfully, Shaun missed it.

Shaun Micheel is one of the quieter tour players, a pedestrian-looking athlete who goes through life largely unnoticed off the course, except when he's hanging out with KISS. Midway through the second round on Thursday, I saw a guy who looked vaguely familiar. A few holes later I realized it was Tommy Thayer, the lead guitarist for KISS. Along with Gene Simmons, Paul Stanley, and drummer Eric Singer, Tommy formed one of the most iconic rock bands in history. I was surprised I recognized him without his makeup, and I was even more astonished to learn that he's an avid golfer and great friend of the Micheels.

"Oh yeah, Tommy plays in my Make-A-Wish tournament every year," Shaun said.

"You have your own Make-A-Wish Foundation tournament?" I asked.

"You bet. You gotta leave the world a better place than you found it."

That quote exemplified Shaun, and a lot of the other pros I had the privilege of befriending. The tour gets a lot of credit for its charitable contributions, but the giving doesn't stop when the tournaments leave town. Players work throughout the year in mostly unheralded ways to make life better for others, a show of character that doesn't get enough attention, in part because players don't make a big deal out of it. These are guys who do good when no one is watching, who still care when the cameras are gone. They aren't the most celebrated athletes on the planet, but they are ones that fathers can point to and say to their son, "There, that man, that's who you should aspire to be."

On Friday, Shaun's pro-am partner was baseball legend Yogi Berra. This twist of fate led to an interesting internal side bet I made with myself. Yogi was eighty-two years old at the time, so on several occasions I had an unofficial race with him down the fairways, even though he was riding in a cart. He didn't know we were racing, of course, which gave me an advantage. He also took his time and waved to hundreds of fans who cheered and yelled his name on every hole. Yogi and I finished in a couple of dead heats, but overall I came out the winner. Too bad he had no idea he was competing with me. I would have loved to get an "It ain't over 'til it's over" out of him.

Shaun finished in the middle of the pack and never contended for the title. I did, however, get to ask him about the biggest moment of his career, the final hole of the final round of the 2003 PGA Championship at Oak Hill. That tournament had become a two-man show between two guys who, at the time, very few people knew. Shaun and Chad Campbell went out on Sunday to duel it out in the final group. It was nip and tuck all day until the final hole, when Shaun put the tournament away with a 7-iron approach that came within an inch of going in the hole.

When he talked about that day, a wistful smile crept into his cheeks, and even though the story had been told many hundreds of times, it looked as though he was reliving it with every breath.

"It's a difficult one to put into words, really," he said, the Memphis drawl seeping in as the story flowed. "It was my first PGA and I was tickled pink just to have qualified. I mean, it's a tough tournament to get in, as are all the majors. I really felt that just making the cut would have been a good start. That was a pretty high goal, just making the cut. Then, as I got going into my rounds I started getting more comfortable with the golf course. It was sort of like Medinah, and I just fell in love with that place. Cary Middlecoff, an old Memphian, won the U.S. Open there. As the days got on, I started thinking about that. Even up until Friday, though I was leading, I really didn't feel like I had a chance to win.

"Then I pretty much decided that I was tired of losing. I was tired of letting my kind of nervous energy affect the way I played and the way I scored. My wife was six months pregnant at the time, and she hadn't really traveled that much because she's an attorney, but she came with me that week. We got to spend some time together, and more than anything I was just comfortable. It was an eerie feeling because I hadn't really felt like that in a long time. I didn't feel nervous. Once

I got going into my round each day I just got into my game. My caddie, Bob, did a great job, and together we just kind of managed the golf course.

"You know, I think everybody's going to remember the shot on the last hole. I mean, I obviously will never forget it. I think what people miss is that I'd played seventy-one pretty good holes prior to that. Looking back I made twenty-one birdies for the week. I mean, I'm not going to make twenty-one birdies at the Bob Hope, and these courses are easy!

"As for the last, it was just a magical, magical way to finish. I can't even describe the feeling. I have a DVD that the PGA of America sent to me and I watch it often. It goes with me everywhere I go, and when I need a pick-me-up, I watch it. I think there's always irony in things, particularly golf. That Tuesday, in my practice round, I got to the eighteenth hole and had basically the same yardage. I think I had one seventy-five, and I hit the same exact club, and it came up just a little bit short, just a little bit into the wind. Then on Sunday I got down from there after hitting a really nice tee ball, and standing over it Bob said, 'You've got one sixty-one and thirteen. Remember on Tuesday you had one seventy-five and came up just a little bit short 'cause there was about a ten-mile-an-hour wind.' I grabbed a 7-iron and it was just the perfect club.

"I don't remember too much about the process of actually hitting the shot. I watch some of the video to try and recapture that. I remember taking a deep breath and just putting the club behind the ball and swinging. I remember my caddie, who never talked to the ball, incidentally—he always knew that was kind of a no-no with me—he's the one on the video you can hear saying, 'Be right!' Everybody thinks it was me saying that. It's not; it was Bob. I just remember thinking in that split second, I cannot believe he's talking to my ball! People always ask me, 'What was going through your mind?' Well, that was what went through my mind. Why is he talking to my golf ball?

"I'm really happy that the ball didn't go in the hole. I feel like if it had gone in, people would have thought, Oh, he won with a lucky shot. But in my mind, a win's a win. It was a great moment, great for me and great for my family."

The week in Palm Springs was great for me and my family as well. Dad traveled with me again, the third of twenty-one weeks we would spend together during my journey. At the time, we were getting a little media attention, blurbs or features in local papers and the occasional segment on local radio, but nothing big. I wasn't looking to become a celebrity, but part of the reason the tour agreed to have me out was the additional publicity they could generate from my presence. So while I didn't wave a flag and shout, "Look at me!" I accommodated any media requests that came my way.

One of those was from the Golf Channel. Producers from the Orlando-based network wanted to shoot a segment with me having dinner with a player. Because I knew his taste in food, I asked Boo Weekley, who jumped at the idea. At first we were going to go to In-N-Out Burger, a Weekley favorite, but the management there wouldn't allow the segment to be shot. The place didn't seem to have any health code problems, and I didn't see anybody in the kitchen who would have immediately raised immigration suspicions. But the manager was emphatic, so we went across the street to Carl's Jr., where the manager said the producers could shoot the segment as long as the camera stayed outside.

Boo and I ended up eating hamburgers in a window booth with a cameraman, producer, sound tech, and my dad standing out in the cool night air watching us through the window.

The Golf Channel people tried to pay, but Boo was having none of it. "These are my friends, and I'm paying," he said.

That moment stuck out because it was the first time one of the players I'd met on this quest called me a friend. It was also the first time a worldwide cable television network ran a segment on what I was doing. Both events turned out to be seminal moments in my unforgettable year.

CHAPTER FIVE

CHASING TIGER

From Palm Springs, the tour moved to San Diego and Torrey Pines, one of the most scenic public golf courses in the world, for the Buick Invitational. Situated on the Pacific, Torrey is always a big event, often the first outing of the year for some of the game's biggest names. But it had an even more electric feel this time around, in part because Tiger Woods had come out of hibernation to make his season-opening debut, and also because a number of players in the Buick Invitational would be back in June when Torrey Pines hosted its first U.S. Open Championship. Everyone wanted to get a look at the course that would host the season's second major.

Steps quickened and speech patterns in the media center took on a more serious tone as Thursday approached. Tiger's presence did more, it seemed, than elevate the play of other professionals; even journalists tended to sharpen their focus when the best golfer in the world showed up.

Fans and objective observers alike wanted to get a glimpse of Tiger. I was no exception. Like everyone who follows sports, I found myself enamored of Tiger. The things he'd accomplished, the records he'd set, the drama he'd created, and the ways he'd elevated golf in the public consciousness were the stuff of legend. Anyone who saw him in person felt the thrill that comes with being a witness to history.

The question I was asked most often during my journey was, "How difficult is it for you to walk every round of every tournament?" The second most asked question was, "Do you think you'll follow Tiger?"

And the third was, "Are you disappointed that you haven't followed Tiger?"

Believe it or not, I wasn't disappointed that Tiger didn't make the D. J. cut. For starters, following Tiger can be a chore. His galleries are like the crowds on Bourbon Street during Mardi Gras. You can't move, you can't see, and you certainly can't get any quality time with the man. His focus on the golf course is just as intense in person as it appears on television. It has to be. He's trying to hit shots and make putts in the middle of a three-ring circus, and he does that job better than anyone else. The only way to liken the challenges Tiger faces to the average person would be for you to imagine the most pressure-packed situation you've ever faced at work, and then imagine having to handle that situation in the middle of the Rose Bowl Parade.

Demands on every tour player are tough; the demands on Tiger are off the charts. Just walking from the parking lot to the clubhouse is a production for him. He has to have security everywhere he goes, he has to have a buffer of guards to walk with him from the clubhouse to the driving range, and he can't grab a hamburger on the way back to his rented house without being mobbed. After his rounds, he is swarmed by autograph seekers and fans who just want to get close to him, and every reporter and photographer wants a sound bite or image, no matter what he shot. In that environment, it's amazing that he can make a cut, much less win as often as he does.

As a lover of the game, I also wanted to show fans that while it's great having the most popular athlete in the world in our sport, the PGA Tour is a lot more than just one guy.

Torrey Pines week, I was fortunate enough to draw Bob Tway, a twenty-three-year tour veteran and former major championship winner. Tway, an Oklahoman and one of the quieter and more thoughtful men on tour, has seen a lot since he made his rookie debut in 1985, so I decided to talk a little golf history with him. For starters, we discussed equipment. "The equipment changes have been the most drastic changes that I've seen," he said. "When I was playing—I am going to date myself here and may sound old—we had wooden drivers and wooden three-woods and the golf ball was totally different. We really didn't have many graphite shafts. As a result of all that, the ball didn't go very far. Dan Pohl led the driving distance back then by hitting it two hundred and eighty yards. I averaged about two sixty-three, which was pretty long at the time. Now a good number of guys average over three hundred yards. Now they keep building longer golf courses to keep up."

"How do you think you would play now with the equipment you had back then?" I asked.

"I don't know that I would play that much different, to tell you the truth," he said. "The equipment change obviously helps a little, but when I learned to play, it was pretty much hit the middle of the face with the driver, and learn to work the ball both ways. We didn't have sixty-degree wedges back then, so you learned to manipulate shots with the wedges. That's probably the number-one difference; we had only fifty-six-degree wedges. Other than that, I would love to go back to the old equipment."

Tway was not alone in that thinking. One of the things I learned in looking into the issue is that nothing is more telling than a thirty-year-old golf magazine. In some ancient issues of *Golf Digest*, I happened upon a couple of features about young up-and-comers like Curtis Strange, Jerry Pate, and Andy Bean. The reason these players were being so highly touted was not their length or strength, but their ability to work the ball. In the days of wooden clubs and rubber golf balls, that was the highest compliment that could be paid to a golfer. Now it's irrelevant. As Stewart Cink told me once, "I've gone back and looked at old footage of past majors, especially those where I might not have played the golf course. What is amazing is how long those courses played as compared to how short they play now. I watched the tape of the 1995 U.S. Open at Shinnecock before playing there in 2004, and couldn't believe how short the course felt when I finally got there. We were hitting two or three clubs less in 2004 than guys were in 1995."

The USGA had been grappling with what they considered an "arms race" with technology for years. Part of that battle was adding length to older courses like Torrey Pines in order to maintain par as a meaningful standard. The course the players face now is 7,600 yards long, the longest on tour. Rees Jones moved a number of the greens closer to the canyons surrounding the course, which made the approaches more difficult, and he added sixty bunkers to the layout. It was a test of length, strength, accuracy, and mental discipline. Even rusty after a winter layoff, Tiger held the advantage on all fronts.

He shot 19 under par and won by a whopping 8 shots.

I spent the weekend with the Weekleys and Baddeleys. When Bob Tway missed the cut, I watched Boo and Aaron, because they played together on Saturday. I felt as though I owed Aaron a debt of thanks for being my guinea pig when I first put my plan together. He had gone out of his way to help me, so I went out of my way to show support for him whenever I could.

"When am I on your schedule officially?" Aaron asked as our weekend in San Diego wound down.

"When do you want me?" I said.

"How about the match play?"

I nodded. "Sounds good. See you then."

Aaron didn't know it at the time, but he had just invited me to stand witness to one of the most exciting golf tournaments in PGA Tour history and one of the best matches ever played.

CHAPTER SIX

THE BEST MATCH EVER

Aaron Baddeley is a lot of things: a multiple tour winner, the youngest golfer ever to win the Australian Open, a history maker when he became the first teenager to successfully defend his country's open, and a young man who has earned a reputation for being the best putter since Ben Crenshaw, maybe the best since Bobby Locke. He's also the son of the former car chief for racing legend Mario Andretti, and a great husband and friend. But more than any of that, Aaron is an unapologetic evangelical Christian, a label he not only accepts but relishes.

"If I weren't a golfer, I'd be a preacher," he said to

me outside a Tucson clubhouse as he was preparing for the first match of the first World Golf Championships event of the year, the WGC-Accenture Match Play Championship. "I love to preach."

The words seemed incongruous coming from such a soft-spoken, innocuous-looking man. A New Hampshire–born Australian with dual citizenship and an Outback-size smile, Aaron reminded me of the quiet kid from high school whom everyone liked but few could remember. He might have gone through life in relative obscurity had he not been gifted with great talent as a golfer. Introduced to the game by both his grandmothers, Aaron broke 80 at age fourteen and never looked back. He won the Australian Open as an eighteen-year-old, then won it again a year later, launching him into the public consciousness as the next great Aussie golfer and a possible challenger to Tiger. The comparisons to Greg Norman, the godfather of modern Australian golf, were inevitable, and while Aaron didn't mind, he was quick to correct anyone who equated him with Greg.

"Greg Norman's got big shoes to fill," he said. "I wouldn't say I feel the pressure to become the next big Australian golfer. I just want to become the best golfer I can become."

By the time we got together in Tucson, he had become very good. After his breakout teenage years, Aaron turned pro and didn't miss a cut on the Australasian Tour. But he hit a slump in America. The swing that had come so naturally to him as a teenager evaporated like mist in the night. He developed what golfers call "the driver yips," a debilitating ailment that causes its sufferers to drive the ball everywhere but in the fairway. Sometimes the problem is mechanical; other times it's psychological.

One of the most famous examples of the driver yips is former British Open winner Ian Baker-Finch, who could drive the ball as straight as a laser on the range and then couldn't find the fairway with a GPS once he teed it up on the course. Baker-Finch retired because of his driving problems, but not before he famously hit a ball out of bounds off the first tee at the

Old Course in St. Andrews, a remarkable feat, given that the fairway was 120 yards wide.

Aaron never got that bad, but he did hit some spectacular hooks before revamping his swing and regaining his confidence. When he didn't earn his PGA Tour card or make it through the final stages of Q-school at age twenty, he spent time on the Nationwide Tour, toiling through a crisis of confidence and largely forgotten by the public. The fact that Aaron rediscovered his game, won twice on the PGA Tour, and worked himself into the top ten in the World Golf Rankings before his twenty-eighth birthday was a testament to his fortitude, maturity, and talent.

"You know, you were the guinea pig for this thing," I reminded him. "It's partially your fault I'm out here. How does it feel to be my player of the week for real?"

"I take zero responsibility for you," he said.

I shook my head. "Too late."

"Glad I could help."

I followed Aaron the week of one of the most

anticipated tournaments on the winter schedule. The Match Play, as it's commonly called, is the only event of the regular golf season that is contested like the majority of golf games played by amateurs. When Harvey plays Joe for two bucks at their local club, they're playing match play, in which one player competes directly against the other, one-on-one, mano a mano. Posting a total score is irrelevant and most times impossible because holes are conceded and gimmes are picked up. Instead of fewer shots taken, the goal is more holes won. It's the most exciting format to watch. The Ryder Cup is match play, and it's the most popular golf event in the world. So when the tour added a sixty-four-player match-play tournament, complete with March Madness brackets and five-round format, players and fans were thrilled.

"I like it; I think having one match-play event is good," Aaron said. "Maybe you could have two, but one is good, something a little different. Unfortunately, if you had two world match-play events, then how do you figure out who wins the world match play?"

The PGA Championship used to be match play, and some have suggested going back. Not only does the head-to-head aspect make for compelling television, it's one of the only formats where early rounds mean a lot. As one fan described it to me, "I watch Thursday and Friday golf the way I listen to Muzak in the dentist's office; it's comforting to have it on, but it's background noise." In match play, every match is critical because you have to win to advance. Just like March Madness, the NCAA college basketball tournament, there are early-round upsets and intense drama from the first shot to the last.

Players gear up differently for match play. When talking about stroke play, Tiger said, "You can't win the tournament on the first day, but you can put yourself in a hole." In match play, coasting for position in the early rounds is not an option. If your opponent gets on a roll in the first round, you have to get on a roll with him. Nobody wants to travel to Arizona on Tuesday only to be eliminated on Wednesday.

Despite the pressure of gearing up for a tough

opening match against Mark Calcavecchia, Aaron gave me all the time I needed. "I wouldn't say I change my preparation for match play, but it changes your mental game or the way you play the golf course. It's straight up, one-on-one, as opposed to playing against everyone else. I mean, you could make an eight on one hole and still win the hole, or make a birdie and lose."

Aaron made plenty of birdies. In his first match he closed Calcavecchia out with a birdie on the sixteenth to end the match four and two. He was gracious and humble in victory, praising his opponent and thanking the sponsors and fans for supporting him before heading off to sign autographs and get ready for round two.

One of the things I learned to do early in my journey was watch how players interact with the fans. I was most interested in unscripted moments. Everyone, it seems, has a public mask, a persona he puts forth at press conferences and other controlled settings. I was on tour long enough to see what players are like when the cameras are off. Aaron, for example, exhibits a quiet calm that is both peaceful and magnetic. People seem drawn to him, not because of his firebrand personality but because of his transparent decency. He is the epitome of Christian goodness, a disciple who spreads his message through his acts. He might have been a good preacher, but from what I could tell, he was a much better ambassador, a man who demonstrated his faith through deeds instead of words.

"Being a Christian definitely plays a big factor in my golf and my life," he said. "It's not all about playing great golf; it's about how you live your life and the example you set outside of golf. I mean, golf's great, but there is more to life."

I also liked what I saw when I looked into Aaron's face. Cerebral palsy keeps me from walking like most people, but my life experience gives me a special acuity, sort of a "spidey sense" for how people react to the disabled. Society has moved beyond seeing the disabled as freaks. Pointing and staring is taboo these days, so reactions are far more nuanced. Some people look away; some tighten their cheeks in an almost imperceptible grimace; others break into big painted smiles while their eyes give off an "oh, how sad" glint of pity.

Celebrities are different, although the trained expert can still pick up on their reactions. When someone in the limelight—whether an actor on the red carpet or an athlete running out for warm-ups—speaks to a disabled person, I always watch to see how much eye contact is made. If a celebrity is more interested in the nearby cameraman than the person he's speaking to, it's a sign. I'm not saying celebrities are disingenuous, but everyone understands the PR benefits of signing an autograph for a kid in a wheel-chair.

In the time I spent with Aaron Baddeley, not only did he not view me as someone with cerebral palsy, he looked at me as a perfect creation of God. In every word and deed that I witnessed, Aaron conducted himself as a servant to a greater power, and he carried himself with the kind of inner peace that impacts everyone who sees him.

Months later, as part of an interview on an unrelated topic, I overheard Aaron say something that struck me. He told the interviewer, "Jesus said, 'That which you do for the least amongst you, you do also for me.' So how we treat those less fortunate is how we are treating Christ in his eyes."

The comment was not directed at me—Aaron didn't even know that I overheard him—but his words pierced me like a rifle shot. Throughout my life I had strived to be seen as normal, to avoid sympathy and never, ever to feel sorry for myself because of my condition. But Aaron's comments, the words he quoted from the Bible, forced me to understand that not acting disabled was not enough. My job, my responsibility, is to lift up those less fortunate than me and serve them accordingly. He didn't realize it at the time, and might not realize it now, but Aaron Baddeley made a point that will stick with me forever. As a physically challenged person, I need to give more to others than was given to me. I've been blessed, so giving better than I've gotten is going to be tough, but if I learned anything from my journey on the PGA Tour, it is that the tougher the test, the more satisfying the victory.

I saw Aaron's potential marquee matchup before the first shot was struck. I'm sure Aaron saw it, too, although he didn't talk about it. The biggest unwritten rule in match play is that you never look past your current opponent. Nothing ensures an upset quicker than focusing on the guy you'll meet tomorrow instead of the guy you're playing today. Aaron didn't do that, but I knew that a win over Calcavecchia followed by a win over David Toms in all likelihood meant that Aaron would meet Tiger Woods in the round of sixteen.

As it turned out, David Toms made the scenario a lot easier by withdrawing with a back injury after his first match. "He must have really been hurting," Aaron said. When Tiger closed out Aaron Oberholser three and two, the Friday game was set. Baddeley and Woods would tee off midmorning in the biggest match of the third round.

It was early in the year, but I had already seen some electrifying golf and experienced the thrill of being in the middle of something special. But nothing could have prepared me for the match between Aaron and Tiger. For starters, I had no choice but to take advantage of my inside-the-ropes credential. The crowds were so thick I wouldn't have seen a shot and might have been trampled if I'd tried to wade through the hordes. I've heard the expression "sea of people," but this was the first time I'd almost gotten seasick from looking at an ocean of roiling heads. They were respectful, but it is impossible to have that many people following one group without some crowd noise. As the match got under way my overriding thought was, *Holy smokes, Tiger puts up with this every time he plays.*

A lot of players crumble when playing with Tiger. Sometimes it's not obvious. They don't tremble or collapse, but they hit more errant shots than normal,

(Above) Boo Weekley and me at the Mercedes-Benz Championship.

(Below) Brandt Snedeker and me at the Sony Open in Hawaii.

Shaun Micheel and me at the Bob Hope Chrysler Classic.

Bob Tway and me at the
Buick Invitational.

(Above) Jeff Quinney and
me at the FBR Open.

Chris DiMarco and me
at the AT&T Pebble Beach
National Pro-Am.

Lucas Glover and me at the Northern Trust Open.

(Below) Me, Aaron Baddeley, Richelle Baddeley, and Pete Bender at the WGC-Accenture Match Play Championship.

Me and Mark Wilson at the Honda Classic.

J.J. Henry and me at
the PODS Championship.

(Above) Kenny Perry, me,
and Sandy Perry at the
Arnold Palmer Invitational
Presented by MasterCard.

My friend Bethany White,
Heath Slocum, and me at
the WGC-CA Championship.

Mark Calcavecchia and me at the
Zurich Classic of New Orleans.

(Above) My mom, Jackie,
Briny Baird, and me at the
Shell Houston Open.

Bubba Watson and me
at the Masters.

Jerry Kelly and me at the
Verizon Heritage.

(Above) Robert Gamez and
me at the EDS Byron Nelson
Championship.

Zach Johnson and me at the
Wachovia Championship.

Jason Bohn and me at the Players
Championship.

(Above) David Duval and me
at the AT&T Classic.

Jim Furyk and me at the
Crowne Plaza Invitational
at Colonial.

Me and Jonathan Byrd at the Memorial Tournament Presented by Morgan Stanley.

(Above) Paul Goydos and me at the Stanford St. Jude Championship.

Me and Stuart Appleby at the U.S. Open.

Me and Steve Marino at the Travelers Championship.

(Below) Me with Team Streelman (Kevin is standing, second from left) at the Buick Open.

Me, Rich Beem, and my friend Doug Wells at the AT&T National.

Peter Lonard and me
at the John Deere Classic.

(Below) Sean O'Hair and me
at the British Open.

Me and Carl Pettersson at the
RBC Canadian Open.

Me and Johnson Wagner at the WGC-Bridgestone Invitational.

(Right) Me and Stewart Cink at the PGA Championship.

Me, Davis Love III, and my sister, Ann, at the Wyndham Championship.

My mom, Ken Duke, me, and Wally (Ken's caddie) at the Barclays.

(Below) Me and Martin Laird at the Deutsche Bank Championship.

Ben Crane and me at the BMW Championship.

(Above) Sharon Funk, me, and Fred Funk at the Viking Classic.

(Right) Dudley Hart and me at the Tour Championship Presented by Coca-Cola.

Me and Woody Austin at the Turning Stone Resort Championship.

Chez Reavie and me at the Valero Texas Open.

Me and Olin Browne at the Frys.com Open.

(Above) George McNeill and me at the Justin Timberlake Shriners Hospitals for Children Open.

(Right) Troy Matteson and me at the Ginn sur Mer Classic.

(Left) My dad, Don, me, and Jason Gore at the Children's Miracle Network Classic Presented by Wal-Mart.

(Below) Meeting Robert Gamez behind the 18th green after the final round of 2008.

Ollie Nutt, tournament director of the AT&T Pebble Beach National Pro-Am, Zach Johnson, me, and Brad Faxon with the PGA Tour plaque that the PGA Tour and players presented me with; it has pictures of all forty-four players I walked with, and each player signed his picture.

(Below) The FootJoy shoes I wore on tour (they had American flag logos on them).

Me with my parents at Verizon Heritage.

To learn more about the players on the PGA Tour, visit www.pgatour.com.

take more time over their putts than usual, catch more bad breaks, hit more lips, and shoot higher scores. My pal Bubba Watson plays a lot of practice rounds with Tiger, in part because they're good friends but also because Bubba wants to get used to the distractions of Tiger crowds in case he's ever paired with him in the final round of a major. The pressure in Tiger's group is always intense. In a match where the winner advances and the loser goes home, it's a pressure cooker.

Early in the match it looked like Aaron would fall victim to the Tiger trap. He hit a couple of tee shots low and left and quickly lost two holes. In an eighteen-hole match, the trick is never to get too far down. If you can keep the match close, anything can happen in the closing holes. That's exactly what Aaron did with some of the best golf of the year. The result was one of the greatest matches in the decade-long history of the WGC-Accenture Match Play Championship.

With back-to-back birdies, Aaron squared the match, and then Tiger pulled ahead. Aaron got the lead back on the final nine, making critical putt after critical putt. They were like two heavyweight fighters slugging it out with their best shots, each man pushing the other to his physical and mental limits. On the final hole Tiger had to make a 10-footer to keep the match all square and force it into extra holes. As he had done on countless occasions, the best player in the world came through in the clutch, rolling the putt into the center of the hole. Both players birdied the nineteenth to keep the playoff going. Then Tiger closed it out with a birdie on the twentieth hole, one Aaron finally could not top.

At the end of a long and dramatic day, Aaron had made ten birdies in twenty holes. Tiger had birdied eleven.

Anyone can be gracious with a win. The fact that Aaron was the same man in defeat that he was in victory said a lot for his character and the example he sets for others. "Sure, I wish I had won, but I played some great golf out there," he said. "If you didn't get a thrill watching this one, you don't have a pulse."

Count me among those who were thrilled. Afterward, Steve Williams, Tiger's caddie and a celebrity in his own right, came up to me and said, "It was great having you out with us today. You brought us luck. Hope you'll stay the rest of the weekend."

I didn't have the heart to tell him I was pulling for Aaron. But I did let him know that he'd be seeing a lot more of me throughout the year.

I took several lessons away from my experience at the match play. For starters, I came to understand that Tiger Woods is not just the greatest golfer in history; he might be the greatest athlete in his sport who ever lived. What I wouldn't know until later is that Tiger was winning with a knee injury that would have sidelined most people, a debilitating ACL tear, the kind of thing that causes football players to be carried off the field on a cart. If you'd written Tiger's year as fiction, it would have been rejected as too unbelievable—a Roy Hobbs–like ending in *The Natural* that would have editors saying things like, "Add a little realism, would you?" I walked away thanking my lucky stars to have stood witness to a year I would be telling my grandkids about for decades to come.

I also learned that while I can be a fan of Tiger's, I do not want to be him. He exists in a world I cannot comprehend, one where I don't think I'd be comfortable. I can, however, aspire to be Aaron Baddeley, a quiet ambassador, a good friend, and a lifetime servant to the least among us: the kind of man every man should want to be.

CHAPTER SEVEN

BECOMING A REGULAR

By March I felt like a tour regular, one of those guys who get a "What's up?" in the locker room and a "See you next week" after the final round. Even players who couldn't recall my name knew who I was and what I was doing. Walking past the putting green, I would always be asked, "Who've you got this week?" or "When are you going to walk with me?"

I was also beginning to understand the enormity of walking two hundred rounds of golf. The blisters on my toes throbbed constantly. Later in the year my hips, calves, thighs, abdominals, feet, hands, shoulders, forearms—heck, everything but my earlobes—hurt. Walking a thousand miles in forty-six weeks might not seem that daunting when you run the numbers; it's just a little over three miles a day, every day; but these weren't three flat miles, and they weren't spread out evenly. Plus, I had all the hassles of traveling; walking through airports, hotels, restaurants; walking around the tournament grounds trying to get my bearings; walking through the clubhouses and media centers; walking from parking lots to shuttle buses to driving ranges to the first tee with my player; and then walking the golf course. I'd been using a cane for most of my life, but for the first time the pad of my right hand felt like it was going to explode from the repetitive pressure.

That turned out to be the least of my aches. The way I walk requires me to stretch my calf muscles more than most people. If you've ever kept your feet flat on the floor and leaned forward against a wall at a twenty-degree angle, you know the burning sensation that comes when the calves are pulled to their limits. Imagine holding that stretch for eight hours.

That's how I walk. Twelve weeks into the season, I realized that my glib responses to "Can you make it?" had been just that: glib and stupid. I was going to have to dig deep to make this thing work.

Thankfully, my circle of support continued to grow. Friends old and new bucked me up with constant encouragement. Patsy Weekley, Boo's mom, kept in e-mail contact when she wasn't out following her son, and Boo always made a point of checking on me when our paths crossed. Just hearing him say, "Keep moving," as I was walking from the range to the first tee put an extra bounce in my step. Months later, Boo would say, "You know, Little Buddy, you were a real inspirator for me, for a bunch of us, really. Watching you out there kept me thinking, you know, people like that, people who love our sport so much that they'd walk a thousand miles when that ain't no easy thang, that was motivatin'."

I'm not sure if he meant "inspiration" or "innovator" but Boo's heartfelt sentiment touched me—and so did the nickname he gave me from *Gilligan's Is-*

D . J .   G R E G O R Y

land. His words and others like them kept me moving when I felt too tired or too sore to go on. At thirty, I might have been at the peak of my manhood, but the boundless energy of youth had already given way to a love of quiet nights and comfortable chairs. A lot of days the only thing that got me out of bed and out to the course was the thought that I can't let these guys down.

The idea that I might be motivating the players, while not something I had ever considered, shot through me like an electrical jolt, one that kept me alert to everything going on around me. A man is blessed with two or three life-changing moments. Unfortunately, many don't realize they are living those moments until it's too late. I knew I was in the middle of my time, and no matter how much fatigue I had to endure, I was going to drink in every second and envelop myself with every sight, sound, smell, and feel from this magical year. I also vowed never to become cynical about what I was doing. If I did nothing else, I would go home a bigger fan of professional golf and a bigger friend of the PGA Tour and its players than when I arrived.

I had no way of knowing that two of the most lasting and meaningful friendships from my yearlong walk would originate in Orlando on week twelve of my quest.

By the time I got to Orlando for the Arnold Palmer Invitational Presented by MasterCard I understood that my story was striking a nerve somewhere. The media snowball was getting bigger by the week. After various news segments on my journey aired, I had requests for radio and television appearances every week. It wasn't long before I understood what players go through and how tough it can be to wear a smile as you're answering the same question for the hundredth time. I remained upbeat by remembering what Boo had said: "No matter how many times you been asked something, they's somebody out there that ain't heard the answer. Ever' day somebody's seeing you for the first time, and how you act 'round 'em is how they're gonna remember you."

Throughout my journey, I thought of those words before I said or did anything in public.

The Monday of Mr. Palmer's tournament at his Bay Hill Club and Lodge, I was smiling my way through another edition of *The Leaderboard Report* on ESPN Radio, a show I did most weeks throughout the year. To my surprise, the producers had arranged for us to be joined by Robert Gamez, a local resident most famous for winning the Arnold Palmer Invitational in his rookie year by holing a 7-iron from the middle of the eighteenth fairway. Fifteen years, three victories, and $6 million in official earnings later, Robert sat down next to me and put on a headset to promote his Robert Gamez Foundation and its annual charity golf tournament to help at-risk kids in central Florida.

I'd never met Robert, although he knew all about me. At the AT&T Pebble Beach National Pro-Am I had walked with Chris DiMarco, and Robert had been fortunate enough to play right behind us the first two days. After watching me hobble up the hills at Pebble Beach, Robert had asked the obligatory "What's that guy's story?" A tour official filled him in. Then his caddie, Mark Huber, approached me and said, "My uncle has cerebral palsy, and I think it's great what you're doing."

I got a lot of those kinds of responses. Many people felt connected to my story in part because cerebral palsy is such an obvious condition, and in part because almost everyone knows someone who has it. A brother, a cousin, a guy you went to school with, or someone you see at church: most people know somebody, either closely or in passing, who deals with cerebral palsy. That connection drew people to me and to what I was doing.

Robert was not one of those people. Other than his caddie's uncle, he didn't know a soul who had cerebral palsy, so he asked all the usual questions. I found his straightforward honesty refreshing. He was curious about my condition, just as I was curious about his golf game. We hit it off immediately. "So when are you going to follow me?" he asked.

"I don't know. When are you playing again?"

He shrugged and said he'd get back to me. Then he said, "I'd love for you to come out to my charity event this week. We've got Hootie and the Blowfish playing a concert on Saturday night, a stand-up comedy night on Sunday, and golf on Monday. Let me know if you can make it."

I thanked him and didn't think any more of it. The invitation seemed spur-of-the-moment, and I didn't want to impose by actually accepting. We shook hands, and Robert said he'd see me out at the course.

It was the start of a friendship that I will treasure for the rest of my life.

My second new friend of the week was also my subject: Kenny Perry, the forty-eight-year-old veteran from Franklin, Kentucky, who, like the last days of a bright nova, made his final professional moments the hottest and most brilliant of his career. Kenny is a humble middle-aged man with a lovely wife and grown children. "I've been married twenty-six years, but sixteen of those I was traveling and she was raising kids, so we're just getting to know one another," he said with a smile.

Sandy Perry smiled, too. They traveled together a lot more once the kids were in college. His son was finishing his senior year at Western Kentucky, Kenny's alma mater, his older daughter had recently gotten her master's at SMU in Dallas and had started a life on her own, while his younger girl was a sophomore at SMU, living in Dallas and completely independent.

"I started golf because of my dad," Kenny said. "Dad was always my biggest fan. He sold insurance, and what time me and him spent together was on the golf course. We'd always spend our weekends playing golf. He would beat the crap out of me and laugh. I gotta tell you, that was tough. I guess my mental toughness comes from my dad. He would beat me so bad, and it'd get me so upset I'd cry. He'd just tear me up. But he did that in everything: board games, cards, whatever. I think he had a master plan to harden me up that way. Now I like it. I've got a quiet killer instinct, something inside of me that wants to win.

"I distinctly remember, I was probably six years old, we had this old bag cover, the one that you would slide over your golf bag and you could snap it on if you wanted. Dad would fill that up with range balls, just old beat-up balls, and I remember Dad would sit on a towel on the ground with a big cigar—he always had a big cigar, still does, and he's eighty-three; I always remember the smoke, the smell, that takes me back to my childhood—but he'd sit there and tee a ball up and I would smack it. Then he'd tee another one up and I'd hit it. Once all the balls were gone, I'd grab that bag cover and take off running down the fairway to pick them all up. Then I'd come back to Dad and say, 'Let's do that again.' He would sit there with me for hours."

I could relate to those stories. My dad sounded like a younger version of Kenny's dad, only instead of pushing me on the golf course, Dad pushed me in school and at home and in every other aspect of life. He knew what I would face; he knew how many times I would be told "you can't do that" and that I would have to be tough and determined to overcome those obstacles. No grade short of an A was acceptable, and there were never any excuses for not doing a job well. "Clean the table and do the dishes" doesn't sound like much of a chore for a kid, unless that kid has one hand on a cane and walks like he's got cement blocks on his feet. Under those circumstances carrying glassware to the sink can be hazardous. But Dad never relented. And like Ken Perry Sr., my dad would stay with me as long as it took for me to reach my goals.

Kenny sat with me for hours as well. He and Sandy took me out to lunch at Five Guys where Kenny went completely unrecognized, just another forty-something golfer enjoying a central Florida vacation. Kenny's caddie was eating with us, and a fan asked him what he was doing in town. When he said he was a tour caddie, the guy said, "Oh, really, for who?"

"Kenny Perry."

The fan shrugged, looked at Kenny, and said, "Who's that?"

"I've had a nice career, a good career," Kenny said. "The majors don't mean that much to me now. I mean, they're important, but that's for the young guys. Now, I spend a lot more time at my golf course, Country Creek. I mean, being raised in the small town of Franklin, Kentucky, 'bout eight thousand people, we had the country club, and I was fortunate that my dad was a member, so I was a clubhouse rat. But my buddies who weren't members didn't get to go out there. I could bring them out two or three times a year, and I just thought that was unfair. It was the only golf course we had, forty miles from Nashville and twenty miles from Bowling Green, and there was nowhere in between to play public golf. I felt like our town needed a golf course. I designed it, built it, opened it in 1995, and haven't drawn a paycheck yet. It's a hard road, but I'm going to keep hanging in there with it. It's a beautiful little golf course, fun to play. It's just something I thought our community needed and I wanted to give back. I hope someday my kids can do something with it.

"I'm always working the counter out there, and people don't recognize me. It's hilarious. One time this gentleman looked me straight in the eye, and said, 'How's Kenny playing this week?' and I said, 'He's playing pretty good.' And, you know, I didn't crack a smile, just took his money and off he went. I looked at my middle sister and we just smiled. It's so funny. I'll have people look at me and say, 'Are you Kenny's brother? You look a lot like him.' But it's a treat being out there. When I'm home, I'm out at that golf course. You can find me there. I'm no different than anybody else. I'm shaking hands, saying hello, and thanking them for coming."

He wasn't quite like everyone else. Kenny married his eighth-grade sweetheart, Sandy, a graduate of Lipscomb University, a Christian college in Nashville. The two set out on a struggling life on the minitours until, five years into his professional career, Kenny earned his tour card. It would be another five years before he would win the Memorial Tournament, hosted by none other than Kenny's idol, Jack Nicklaus. The win didn't come easy, even after Kenny shot a course-record 63 at Muirfield Village. Hale Irwin put together a career weekend and forced a playoff, which Kenny won with a birdie on the first extra hole.

From there he became a steady, not great, performer. He won again in 1994 at the New England Classic, and he won the Bob Hope in 1995. But with success came disappointment. When the PGA Championship came to Kentucky for the first time in 1994, Kenny had a two-shot lead at Valhalla with one hole to play. He bogeyed the eighteenth, which allowed Mark Brooks to catch him with a birdie. One hole later (the last time the PGA Championship was decided in sudden death) Brooks had earned his only major, and Perry had to live with one of the biggest disappointments of his career.

He would win six more times in the next decade, but as he put it, "I've always had a little lazy dog in me. It's been a nice career, but I'm not the guy you pick out as being one of the greatest."

Maybe not on the golf course, but in many ways there are no better pros than Kenny.

"When you give back, that's the best thing, much better than the wins. I tried to make the tour a couple of times, and I struggled. My wife and I, we'd just had a child, and I went to an elder in my church, and I said, 'Ronnie, I need five thousand dollars to go to the qualifying school one more time.' I'd missed making the tour by a shot in 1984, and in 1985 my son was born during the fourth round of the finals, so I had to bail and run back to Vero Beach and watch him being born. So, in eighty-six, I asked this church elder for help.

"That man taught me one of the greatest life lessons I've ever learned. He had two boys in college, and I didn't figure he had the money, but he said to me, 'I'm going to give you the money, and here's what we're going to do: If you don't make it through qualifying school, you don't owe me a dime. But if you make it, I want you to give a percentage of your earnings back to Lipscomb University.'

"It was amazing how God just seemed to take over at that point, because I just breezed right through all the qualifiers. I've given five percent of my earnings back to Lipscomb University ever since. So far, I've made about twenty-two million on tour, which is hard to believe, so more than a million dollars has gone to a trust at Lipscomb.

"Our goal was that in Simpson County, Kentucky, if any kid wanted a Christian education, it would be taken care of; money wouldn't be an issue. Lipscomb costs about twenty-six thousand a year. So far we've had twenty-six kids from Simpson County receive this scholarship. If they want to go to Lipscomb, I want to make sure that opportunity's there.

"It's been a neat blessing."

Befriending the Perrys was a neat blessing for me as well. Any week that Kenny played, he would find me. "You gettin' along all right?" he'd ask, and we would talk for a few minutes. He kept track of how many miles I'd walked and wanted to know how many times I'd fallen and if I'd had any problems. "I love you like a brother," he said to me more than once.

In many ways he was better than a brother. No sibling I know would ever offer to give up Ryder Cup tickets.

Months after our first meeting Sandy sent me a text message that said, "We have Ryder Cup tickets for you. Please come." Word had filtered back to Kenny that I wasn't planning on being in Louisville for the Ryder Cup, in part because it is a PGA of America, not a PGA Tour, event (and the two organizations don't always get along). Also, the Viking Classic was being played in Mississippi at the same time. When events conflicted, I felt obligated to stay with the PGA Tour, the organization that had made my year possible.

It was a hard decision. The friends I'd made, guys like Kenny and Boo, wanted me to be in their corner at the Ryder Cup. But I knew that I couldn't take

Kenny's tickets. He was a native Kentuckian with dozens of relatives and thousands of friends wanting to watch him. The offer was extraordinary, one that I would never forget, but I had to turn him down. The tournament meant too much to him for his family to miss it.

Kenny had thought about retiring. Then the PGA of America announced Valhalla outside Louisville as the site of the 2008 Ryder Cup. Suddenly, Franklin's Finest had a reason to play, a goal that would put a final exclamation point on his career.

"My goals have changed over time," he said after the season was over. "I don't have any more mountains. This Ryder Cup was my ultimate goal. I'd only played in one in 2004 and it was the worst experience of my life—we got beat so bad and I didn't get to play much. So this one was a dream. I didn't think I'd get to play. I heard Paul Azinger say, 'You've got to win to get on my team.' I knew I was going to have to step it up, but that was my goal, and to have the summer I did to put me on the team just really blew me away."

That summer included a win at the Memorial Tournament, Jack Nicklaus's event in Ohio, where Kenny got his first professional win. He wasn't playing in the final group on Sunday, but he had the low round of the day, shooting 69 to win by 2 over Justin Rose and Jerry Kelly. When he walked off the final green, I was waiting for him by the scoring hut. He hugged me and thanked me for hanging around to watch him. Then he invited my dad and me to have dinner with him, Sandy, and his family in the clubhouse after the trophy ceremony and obligatory media interviews. During that dinner he turned to me and said, "It really means a lot to me that you stayed around to see this."

It meant even more to me, especially given what that win would ultimately mean for Kenny's career. He made no secret of his intentions. He geared his schedule around making the Ryder Cup team, which, to him, meant skipping the British Open and playing in Milwaukee, where he thought he had a better chance to win, a decision that earned him a level of scorn he'd never experienced. Even Peter Dawson, secretary of the Royal and Ancient Golf Club of St. Andrews, said, "Well, I'm bemused by it more than anything else, really. It's his decision what he does with his life, not mine, but he's in incredibly hot form. He's forty-seven or forty-eight years old. You would have thought he'd never have a better chance, and he's choosing another route." Then Dawson shook his head and said, "We're sorry he's not here."

"I proved 'em wrong, didn't I?" Kenny said later, a huge grin bursting onto his face. "They're eating crow right now. I love stuff like that. They didn't understand me. They didn't understand the purpose I have in my life. If you've never played in a Ryder Cup, you can't understand. You're playing for your country, for your team, your fans, your family and friends, and your captain. My whole life has been selfish, playing a game for myself, setting goals for myself. To have eleven other guys playing with you, wanting you to play great, and a coach pumping you up, that was what motivated me, what got me going.

That's why I did what I did. This was going to define my career. I knew that six hundred million people would see this Ryder Cup around the world; it's the biggest stage in golf. So I said, 'Cinderella might not find the slipper, but it won't be for lack of trying.' Yeah, a lot of people questioned that. But nobody's questioning it now."

Once he made the team, Kenny traveled to Valhalla—the spot where his only legitimate shot at a major slipped through his fingers—to get a sense of what it was going to be like, to see if all the effort and sacrifice had been worth it. "I went in a week earlier and saw the grandstands and the setup. I knew how special it was going to be."

Nobody could have predicted the atmosphere, though. "As many years as I've been playing and as many tournaments as I've played, I've never seen a theater like that," Kenny said. "It was unbelievable. All the British chants and the Americans firing back at them. That 'London Bridge Is Falling Down' song was one of the funniest things I've ever heard. Their little song was, 'What are you going to do without your Tiger?' But I gotta admit they killed us in singing. I guess all those nights in the pubs, they learn to sing 'em some songs."

The atmosphere got even crazier after American team captain Paul Azinger and the PGA put together a pep rally in downtown Louisville. "We went down to Fourth Street and I felt like a rock star," Kenny said. "We're behind the stage, and Zinger goes running out. We were right behind him, throwing T-shirts and towels. It was like the ball drop on New Year's Eve. People shoulder to shoulder as far as you can see. Zinger was screaming out the introductions. We got really fired up.

"It didn't slow down after that. There were so many Kentucky people out there it was unbelievable. I've never heard so many people yell, 'Go, Hill Toppers.' I'm a Western Kentucky guy, so I'm sure J.B. Holmes got a lot of 'U.K.' and 'Go, Cats' chants, but I got a lot of people yelling 'WKU' and 'Hill Toppers.' The Ryder Cup, you've got like ten thousand people on every hole. Every hole felt like the eighteenth hole of a tournament you're trying to win, only louder."

They were especially loud for Kenny and J.B. Holmes, native Kentuckians who were as removed from the glitzy life of the superstar athlete as you could get. "We're working guys just like the fans," Kenny said. "There's no flash about us. We're just normal folks. Fans saw that and appreciated it."

The crowd showed their love all week. "I felt like the governor out there waving to everybody," Kenny said. "Every hole was great. Normally when I do that, my mind wanders and I can't get back in the moment to hit the next shot. But for some reason this week I was able to step out, enjoy the crowd, wave to everybody there, and then step back in and turn my focus to tunnel vision."

That tunnel vision resulted in two and a half points for Team America in four matches, capped off by an emphatic singles victory against Sweden's Henrik Stenson.

Nervous as a cat, Kenny called his opponent

"Henry" most of the day, but nobody found that malicious. "He's a really good guy and we had a great match," Kenny said. "On the seventh tee he looked at me through those dark glasses and said, 'You're not going to make it easy on me, are you?' I said, 'Henry, I like you; you're a good guy; but this is my swan song. I'm playing as hard as I can.'"

The match was essentially over when Kenny sank a 12-footer for birdie on the fifteenth hole. Three up with three holes to play, an easy par on sixteen sealed it.

"It was the greatest gift I could have ever given my father," Kenny said. "His passion is golf. For him to see me in that environment, and come walking on that green at nearly eighty-five years old—I mean, he looked like the cat that swallowed the canary. I couldn't hold back the tears. It was really a neat, neat deal."

The Perrys celebrated with everyone else, albeit in a more subdued manner. "I don't drink, although I did take a sip of champagne when we toasted. But the Europeans came down and joined us about one thirty in the morning. We all hugged and talked, and they partied hard. Now, those guys know how to have a good time! The wives were great, too. They all came up and congratulated us. They left at about four. That's when I left, but I couldn't sleep. Sandy and I got up at about seven and drove home, about an hour and a half, a good amount of time for me to think about what had just happened."

What he later said he realized was that he couldn't have scripted a better ending to his career. Nobody could.

"If I never hit another shot, what a way to go out! I remember the words of my son. He played at Western Kentucky and they had their conference tournament at the Robert Trent Jones Trail in Alabama. I think he shot seventy-four, seventy, and sixty-five on some tough courses. After he was done he looked at me and said, 'Dad, that's a great way to go out!' Those are the words that kept coming into my mind. This was a great way to go out.

"It was my swan song. I had thought this Ryder Cup would be the high point in my career, but I was wrong. It made my career."

At Bay Hill, Kenny made the cut but had a so-so week, finishing tied for forty-eighth. Tiger won again, this time draining an impossible putt for birdie on the final hole, a highlight reel shot where he threw down his hat to the roars of the crowd.

The biggest surprise for me was not the outcome of the tournament or the way Kenny played, but the invitation I got during the final round. Robert Gamez's caddie, Mark, found me on the sixteenth fairway as I was watching Kenny hit his approach.

"Robert has a spot open in his tournament, and he'd really like you to play," Mark said.

"Yes, absolutely, sure, I'd love to," I said.

"Perfect, and come to the comedy show, too. It's always great."

"Yeah, can't wait," I said, still somewhat stunned. "Tell Robert thanks, thanks a lot."

"No, thank you," Mark said. "There's a lot of interest in your story. You'll be a good draw for the field."

That was when I knew things had changed. A few months prior, I was the guy on the golf course with the cane and the limp, the one who played one-handed from the forward tees and never broke 100; the guy who drew quizzical stares on the first tee and who elicited groans from the group scheduled to play behind him. Now I was being invited to a charity event because I would be "a good draw for the field."

Set a goal and don't let anyone distract you from it. Figure out a way. Put blinders on and do whatever it takes to turn your dreams into a reality. There is no force stronger than the force of will. Those were the traits that made Kenny's year so special, and they were part of the reason we became such firm and fast friends. Kenny Perry and I traveled parallel paths during our year together on tour. Like Kenny, I set a goal and put the blinders on, never letting anyone stop me from fulfilling my dream.

Listening to Kenny was like listening to myself. The lessons of his life are the ones I hope to share through mine. Stick it out. Never give up. Don't let others define you. Kenny did it. I did it. You can do it, too.

CHAPTER EIGHT

THINGS YOU'VE NEVER SEEN

The tour was kind enough to provide me with two credentials to each event, which allowed my dad to travel with me for twenty-one weeks. Mom went to nine tournaments, and I asked friends to tag along the rest of the time. Not that I couldn't travel on my own. I'd trekked the country alone for years, but it was great to have someone along to share in this once-in-a-lifetime experience.

It also gave my friends a chance to experience things they wouldn't otherwise see, like Augusta National Golf Club and the Masters.

What many casual observers don't realize is that golf has four majors—the Masters, the U.S. Open, the British Open (the oldest golf tournament in the world), and the PGA Championship—and the PGA Tour has nothing to do with any of them. The U.S. Open is run by the United States Golf Association, the guys who write the *Rules of Golf* and tell you which clubs are legal; the British Open falls under the purview of the Royal and Ancient Golf Club of St. Andrews; the PGA Championship belongs to the PGA of America; and the Masters, the first major of the season and the youngest of the four, is an invitational put on by the members of Augusta National. The PGA Tour, the most popular and powerful organization in the game, plays no role in golf's four biggest events, a matter of some consternation among tour officials.

As a follower of the game, I knew the tour didn't operate the majors, but it wasn't until I got to Augusta that I realized what that meant. My credentials for the Masters weren't the same as the ones I'd gotten at every regular tour event, and, like everyone who entered the hallowed grounds of Augusta National, I walked on pins and needles in fear of doing something wrong and being politely but firmly escorted from the premises.

Golden chalices from the table of Vespasian aren't as coveted as credentials to the Masters. Tickets have gone for as high as $10,000, and, in the past, companies have dropped seven figures renting houses and bringing in clients for the week. The fact that my friends at the PGA Tour finagled two credentials for me was nothing short of a star-in-the-East miracle. When word spread through my inner circle that I had two badges for Masters Week, every person I'd ever known became my best friend.

I asked Kelly Thompson, the assistant women's basketball coach at Stonehill College, a Division II school in Easton, Massachusetts, if she would like to go to Augusta with me. I might as well have said, "I've got this extra Ferrari out front and I was wondering if you'd take it off my hands." When the cheers, hoots, screams, and whistles died down, I said, "I take that as a yes."

"Why me?" Kelly asked after she caught her breath.

"We're teammates," I said. "And you take me to the Final Four every year, something I'd never get to do otherwise. The Masters is something you wouldn't see otherwise."

"Does this mean I owe you?"

"Permanent loyalty and praise."

"I'm not worthy to touch the hem of your garment."

"That's enough out of you."

This was typical of our banter. After all, we were teammates.

For obvious reasons I could never play organized sports, a fact that didn't bother me other than occasionally feeling like I'd missed out on some channels for my natural competitiveness. My father was a different story. He would have disemboweled himself with a dull sword before ever saying he was disappointed in me. He never hinted it and probably never thought it. But for a former two-sport college athlete, a track star and a wide receiver on the only undefeated team in Springfield College history, there had to be some wistful moments. He was never able to throw a football with me in the yard, never could teach me a crossover dribble, or buy matching baseball gloves or hockey gear, or coach my soccer team. He was never able to wear a goofy homemade button of me in ill-fitting shoulder pads or cheer after I made a tackle or a free throw or simply ran out onto the field for warm-ups. He certainly made the best of our time together. As a child I never wanted for anything and never once sensed my father mourning what might have been. Still, I knew he longed for that competitive connec-tion, that athletic bond he'd known throughout his own youth. I also wanted to be where the action was, so in my sophomore year at Springfield I interviewed to be the manager of the women's basketball team.

Dad was surprised. Then he was thrilled. As a member of the board of trustees at Springfield, he had always been vested in the success of the school's athletic teams. When I became team manager for the women, he became the unofficial team dad. He flew to Massachusetts for trustee meetings and took the entire team out to dinner. "It's like I gained fourteen extra children," he always said, loving every minute of it. Before the scores were posted in the newspapers or on the Internet, Dad knew whether or not the Springfield women had won, because I called him after every win. If he didn't get a call, he knew we lost.

Coach Naomi Graves was one of the best bosses and best coaches I could have had. I worked for her for five years, from my sophomore season throughout graduate school, doing scouting reports, game stats, and uniform checks, and getting everything ready for road trips. The players, my teammates, became some of my best friends. I even lived with eight of them. During their senior year and my second year of grad school, some of the women were concerned that the best on-campus housing might fill up before their names got drawn, so they asked me if I'd consider rooming with them.

"Sure," I said. Eight girls, one guy. I might have cerebral palsy, but I'm not stupid. "If you don't mind me asking, why me?"

One of the girls said, "Because the best apartment building's the one that's handicap accessible."

"And you need me for the gimp rule!" I said.

"Exactly."

Those women remain some of my best friends to this day. Kelly Thompson, a tenacious shooting guard with a mean fadeaway, was one of them.

I had been Kelly's guest at the Women's NCAA Final Four every year since she'd gone into coaching. The Masters was my chance to return the favor.

No matter how wonderful Augusta National looks on television (even in HD) and no matter how many breathless adjectives Jim Nantz and his colleagues at CBS come up with to describe it, the place is even more beautiful still. The fact that it's tucked behind a magnolia wall off Washington Road, next to a strip mall and Hooters, only adds to the mystique of the place. Walking through the gates is like falling through golf's magic looking glass. Everything on one side is grim and commercial, and everything on the other is green and manicured.

I had been warned about Augusta. "It's hillier than you think" and "It's a tough course to walk" were two of the cautionary snippets. The elevation changes were, indeed, a lot steeper than they appeared on TV, but it was like a gently rolling meadow, compared to Kapalua. Maybe it was the excitement that came with seeing some of golf's holiest sights—the oak tree behind the clubhouse where the rich and famous from business, sports, and entertainment gathered; the Eisenhower cabin with the presidential eagle still hanging over the door; Amen Corner, the most beautiful and dramatic stretch of holes in the world; and the par-3 course where Jack Nicklaus, Arnold Palmer, and Gary Player paired up to thrill the galleries one more time—or maybe it was the adrenaline that came with walking on Bobby Jones's masterpiece, but I had no trouble at all getting around the place.

My subject for the week was Bubba Watson, a left-handed Floridian who was locked in a battle with J.B. Holmes for the title of longest hitter on tour. Bubba had a long swing reminiscent of John Daly's, when John was ten years younger and thirty pounds lighter. The other difference: John hit the ball 300 yards in his prime; Bubba regularly bombs it 350. Just to rub it in a little, the otherwise gentlemanly Bubba had a pink shaft in his driver. "It's just for fun," he said. "I like bright colors and if I outdrive you with a pink-shafted driver, well, you can't really make fun of it, can you?"

Nobody made fun of the self-taught kid from Bagdad, Florida. He was one of the top sixty players in the world and the second-best athlete in his immediate family. In the par-3 contest, a Wednesday ritual on the nine-hole par-3 course, Bubba's wife, Angie, caddied for him. If it had been a footrace instead of a golf tournament, Angie probably would have won. A college basketball player, Angie was the best athlete in the Watson household, a fact Bubba readily admitted.

"I think if we played one-on-one basketball right now I might win because she hasn't played in a long time, but when we first met, she beat me all the time," he said. "Now, she plays golf and loves it. I didn't teach her or anything. I just gave her some clubs and told her to go hit balls and figure it out. That's the way I learned and that's the way you learn. You hit it, figure out why it went a certain way, and hit it again. She's getting pretty good."

Bubba got pretty good himself using his own advice, which made him a fan favorite. "I don't know if I'm one of the most popular players out here, but the fans that like me, they like me because they can see that I'm not going to change," he said. "I am who I am. I'm not out here with all my coaches around: my strength coach, my mental coach, my swing coach. People see that I enjoy the game. That's why I play. If

I play well, I want it to be because of me; if I play bad, it's because of me. I'm not going to blame it on my caddie, blame it on my coaches, I'm not going to do any of that, it's all on me. I hope people see that and appreciate it."

They appreciated him all week in Augusta. I couldn't tell if the enthusiastic reception he got on the first tee was because of his popularity as a tour pro or because he was a former Bulldog from the University of Georgia. Athens was just ninety miles from Augusta, and a good number of Masters patrons were Georgia fans. Either way, Bubba got more than his share of cheers, along with a few gasps as he launched tee shots that looked like they were never going to come down.

"I like to cut my driver off the tee and there are a lot of cut drivers out here," Bubba said. "If I can putt well, I might catch a break."

Putting well is always the key to scoring well at Augusta. Bubba rolled his putts okay, but okay doesn't cut it at Augusta National. He finished the week 3 over par and tied for twentieth. South African Trevor Immelman had the best putting week of his career and held off Tiger Woods to become the surprise winner of the Masters tournament.

I tried to see and do as much as possible during my week. I asked questions of everyone. The first: What's the big deal with the pimento cheese sandwiches? Well, Clifford Roberts, the first chairman of Augusta, who ran the place with the kind of iron fist that would make Uncle Joe Stalin stand up and applaud, loved pimento cheese on white bread, and he made sure that the concessions promoted them accordingly. For years during Roberts's reign, eighty percent of the stories about the sights and sounds of the Masters mentioned the exquisite and modestly priced pimento cheese sandwiches. The stories are mercifully gone, but the sandwiches remain.

And why are the crowds (they're "patrons," not galleries at Augusta) always called "the most knowledgeable and courteous in golf"? That one was easy:

The tickets are such precious commodities that people on the "patron" list are always on their best behavior. There's no running at Augusta, not because the fans don't want to scramble ahead and see their favorite players but because if you break into anything resembling a trot, a Pinkerton security guard will snatch away your badge, lead you by the elbow to the nearest gate, and belch you out of Wonderland and back onto Washington Road.

I failed to learn the reason for the yellow hard hats worn by all the Masters volunteers. "There is no reason," one of the volunteers told me one night at Outback. I recognized the guy from the fifth hole earlier in the day. "There's no story behind it, but everybody wears one and you have to turn it in at the end of every day. I've been doing it twenty years and you get the same hat every year. They don't even buy new ones. I had a guy offer me five hundred dollars for it, but there's no way I'd sell it. The second you lose it, you lose your spot on the volunteer rolls. No way am I risking that."

"But it's a volunteer job, right? You don't get paid for it."

"No, but you get to see the Masters, and you get to play the course one day a year."

For a round of golf at Augusta, the indignity of wearing a twenty-year-old hard hat is a small price to pay. Any fan of golf would understand completely.

The Masters is not just the most majestic golf tournament in the world; it is one of the most exciting and certainly the best run. The members at Augusta National don't put up with any nonsense, but they also put on the best show in sports, the crown jewel of golf, an event any true fan would give an appendage (or at least a tooth or two) to see in person.

I fell only once, on Friday, as I walked down the hill after Bubba's opening tee shot of the second round. That was one less time than Angie Watson, who took a couple of tumbles on the wet pine straw as she tried to keep up with her husband. It also equaled the number if not the quality of falls by Patsy Weekley, who made a point of tracking me down and showing me her mud-caked backside after taking another spectacular spill in some of Augusta's more organic material.

Kelly got a kick out of some of the players and their families' obsession with seeing me fall. Bubba seemed genuinely upset that I'd taken a slight header down one of the hills and he'd missed it. "One of the goals for the rest of this year is seeing you fall," he told me afterward.

Kelly and I were both a little taken aback by the number of people who approached me during the week. By Friday, at least a dozen strangers had told me that they'd seen my story on television or read about me in the papers or online. Before the week was out that number would double. Three people in one day actually asked for my autograph. "You're really an inspiration," one woman said as I signed her pairing sheet. "Keep it up. We're all pulling for you."

As we walked back down the fairway, Kelly was quiet for a few seconds. Then she said, "Wow, Deej."

"Yeah, it's pretty crazy, isn't it?"

She stopped and looked at me. "What you're doing here's important, Deej. It's not just about you living out your dreams. Not anymore. These people are drawing strength from you. You can't let them down."

Spoken like a spunky guard who played well beyond her talent and who now coached other young athletes to do the same thing.

"Don't worry," I said. "I'm here for the duration."

"You better be," Kelly said. "We're counting on you."

CHAPTER NINE

ADDED PRESSURES

Life is full of curveballs. One of the most important lessons I've learned from living with cerebral palsy is that no matter how much easier things
seem to go for your neighbors, in truth you probably
wouldn't swap problems with them for a million
bucks. I've met countless able-bodied people who
have gone through a lot tougher trials than I could
ever imagine, and I have countless acquaintances
with troubles so deep they would swap places with
me in a heartbeat. *You mean I can have cerebral palsy
and all the rest of this stuff will go away? Where do I
sign up?*

Every life runs off the rails at some point. Nobody sails through unscathed. The questions aren't "Am I going to have struggles and heartache?" They are "How tough will my troubles be?" and "How will I respond to them?"

I'm no therapist or theologian, but my answer has always been: Keep putting one foot in front of the other, take the next breath and next step, and never, ever, ever give up. No matter how much you are suffering or struggling, there have been people before you who had it a lot worse and handled it a lot better. Keep moving and keep doing; things will eventually turn in your favor. It's not an earth-shattering revelation, but it is the truth. Persistence is the key to overcoming the tremors of life. I wasn't dealt a hand full of aces, but I sometimes think my difficulties have been a blessing. I've never known any other way of living. Others, people who have had everything and lost it, suffer more and have to overcome more than I ever have.

That fact came crashing home to me when I visited Walter Reed Hospital during the week of the AT&T

National in suburban Washington, D.C. As someone who went through physical therapy growing up, I'd seen my share of hospital rehab centers. I'd also been around plenty of amputees. What I hadn't seen were young men and women whose lives had been forever altered by the brutality of war. Those heroes, many learning to live without arms or legs, personified the never-stop attitude that I believe is essential to a happy and fulfilling life. Most of the soldiers, sailors, and marines I spoke to at Walter Reed talked about returning to active duty after they learned how to get along with their new prosthetics. I had never been so moved, and may never be again.

Persistence is the mortar that holds the bricks of life in place. And it is the persistent person who overcomes adversity and thrives again, no matter what he's been through. I think persistence is what attracted me to golf, since it is not a game dominated by talent alone. The biggest, strongest, and fastest people aren't the most dominant golfers. In fact, tour pros don't reach the upper tier of their sport because of their genes; they reach the pinnacle of their chosen sport through endless hours on the range and by digging themselves out of the wells of disappointments and pressing on, even when the game has beaten them down.

No golfer personified that never-give-up attitude better than my friend Robert Gamez.

After playing in his tournament in Orlando, I saw Robert again on Hilton Head Island at the Verizon Heritage. "When are you following me?" he asked.

"When are you playing?"

"Dallas," he said. "The Nelson." This was tour shorthand for the EDS Byron Nelson Championship, one of only two tournaments named after former players, the other being the Arnold Palmer Invitational. Jack Nicklaus's tournament is called the Memorial, but Jack's name isn't in the title, and even though Tiger hosts the AT&T National and an unofficial challenge event, the Chevron World Challenge, he doesn't put his name in the header of either. The EDS Byron Nelson chose to keep Mr. Nelson's name to honor one of the all-time great players and legendary gentlemen of the game.

It was the perfect event for me to follow my newest friend. I followed Robert at the TPC Las Colinas Four Seasons Resort in the home of the Dallas Cowboys, Irving, Texas. It turned out to be one of the seminal moments of my year, because it solidified my friendship with one of the nicest guys I've ever met.

Robert Anthony Gamez was a Vegas kid, born in the city's heyday, a time of the Rat Pack, the Stardust, and Cadillacs with trunks that would hold two dead bodies and a full-size spare. "I picked up my first golf club when I was two years old," Robert said. "My dad was supposed to be babysitting me while Mom worked, so he took me out to the range and plopped me down on one end while he hit some balls. All of a sudden I picked up his club and started whacking balls. Dad liked what he saw, so he cut down a little 3-iron for me, and I started hitting balls in the backyard. I got my first set of junior clubs at the age of five, and it took off from there."

A stud at the University of Arizona, Robert was the college player of the year in 1989. "David Toms and I were neck and neck at the end of the year," he said. "We tied at the NCAA Championship, which gave me a little bit of an edge. If he'd beaten me there, he would have been player of the year. Being honored that way was pretty cool, though."

Then Robert did something that has been done only four times in history. He came out of college and won in his first professional start at the Northern Telecom Open. "The great thing was it was in Tucson at Star Pass, a golf course we played in college twice a week, so I knew it like the back of my hand," he said. "I had a six-shot lead going to the last hole and made a smooth double bogey to win." Then he laughed, shook his head, and said, "I tell you what, that was a great time to win. I had just finished school in eighty-nine and had a ton of people out there watching me. It was just a blast."

He won again that same year at Bay Hill, and just like that, Robert Gamez was being touted as the Next

Big Thing. Not since Ben Crenshaw won right out of college and brought a David Cassidy–size horde of nubile female fans onto the tour had a rookie generated so much buzz. At a time when Tiger Woods was a geeky high school freshman with thick glasses, the buzz in golf centered on Robert.

Then, just as quickly as his star had risen, he fell. It would be fifteen and a half years before he would win again, a tour record for elapsed time between wins. During that seemingly endless drought, he would lose his card, earn it back, get in a car crash, finish second a couple of times, and struggle with his putter, his driver, his confidence, and his temper. But never in that time did he consider giving up. Quitting was simply not in his nature.

"I never doubted that I'd win again," he said. "It was tough; going that long between wins was a hard thing. I won Tucson, and then won at Bay Hill by holing a shot on the last hole to beat Larry Mize and Greg Norman. I'll tell you what: I thought this game was easy, so I stopped practicing. I didn't practice as hard and I had too much fun, partied a little bit, enjoyed my life out here on tour, and just never thought I'd have trouble winning golf tournaments. Then my putter started leaving me; I started losing confidence in it. And if you lose confidence in your putter out here, that's the kiss of death. Winning on tour is all about making putts. Everybody hits the ball about the same. Tee to green is not much different, but when you start missing two- and three-footers for pars, and you start lagging longer birdie putts, really not trying to make them, you're in deep trouble. That was me for a while.

"I had some good things happen in 2005 where I had a couple of chances to win. In 2002, it seemed like every week I had a chance to win and struggled on Sunday and finished around twentieth. I just wasn't quite hitting on all cylinders, not driving it real well, not as confident as I should have been. Then the week before the Valero Texas Open in 2005, I missed the cut by a few shots and made a couple of bad swings, made a couple of doubles, but I knew I was playing well—I just wasn't driving the ball real well. So I took the weekend off and worked hard on my driver. When I got to San Antonio, a place that I love with a lot of family there and a golf course I love as well, I entered the week thinking, This is it. I can turn this thing around and win.

"The time between wins didn't enter my mind. Valero has always been great since they took over the tournament. I love the golf course, even though you have to drive the ball well, which I hadn't been doing. But I just felt comfortable from the start. It's funny, because on Monday of that week, I saw the trophy being brought into the press tent as I was walking toward registration. Whoever brought the trophy in asked me if I wanted to grab it. I said, 'No, I'll just grab it on Sunday after I win.' That's just how I felt. It's weird when you have those feelings, even after you've missed the cut the week before and really don't have anything going right. It was a great feeling, even though going that long between wins was tough. It made it that much sweeter when it happened."

He never wavered, never quit. Imagine working on a goal for fifteen years and never quite making it. The close calls would become like torture, a haunting prize that was just out of reach. Most people would call it quits after a decade or so. But Robert kept putting one foot in front of the other, kept tinkering and toiling, working on his game, striving to improve even when all seemed lost. He never lost sight of his dream, and he never, ever let the urge to quit overpower him.

Robert didn't play particularly well in Irving, which was beginning to make me feel uncomfortable. For a little more than a month I hit a stretch where everyone I followed missed the cut. Robert gakked a couple of short putts during Thursday's opening round, and he hit his tee shot in the water on the third hole, leading to a double bogey. He finished the first round at 3 over and tied for eighty-seventh. A lackluster 2 over par on Friday where no putts fell left him two shots outside the cut line.

The temper flared only once. Knowing that he

needed a couple of birdies to play the weekend, he pushed an approach shot well right of the pin on his penultimate hole. That led to a bad word and a back-handed swat of his golf bag with the offending iron, the kind of thing that probably cost him a few hundred dollars in fines from the tour but that would have won him Mr. Congeniality in my normal group.

Afterward, he found me standing by his wife, Lynn, behind the eighteenth green. He hugged me and said, "I really wanted to make the cut for you. I felt like I put extra pressure on myself, because I wanted to do well for you."

"For me! Jeez, Robert, you're not out here for me."

"I know," he said. "The fact that you're out here for us . . . Anyway, I wanted to play well with you out here."

"You'll play great next week," I said. "That's the way it's been working. Anybody who misses the cut while I'm watching plays great the next time out."

"That's good to know."

Then he put his arm around Lynn, turned back to me, and said, "We're still on for dinner Saturday night, right?"

I was taken aback for a second. He'd just missed the cut, so I assumed he would be on the next flight back home to Orlando. "You're hanging around?" I asked.

"I am if you're still going to eat with us."

I had to turn away and blink my eyes before answering. I had lifelong friends who would have blown me off for dinner in a heartbeat after a couple of hard days at work. Canceling never occurred to Robert, a fact that spoke volumes about his character, and his commitment not just to me, but to everything he did.

"I'll be there," I said.

He smiled and nodded as he walked away and said, "So will I."

CHAPTER TEN

ROLE MODELS

Mr. D.J. Gregory inspired me, because I want to be a second-grade math teacher, but I always had worries about college, if I could do the job, and if I had the patience. Now, I feel that I can reach my goal if I have confidence and determination. My goal is to be a teacher in Maine and be a mother of two twin boys.

I want to thank D.J. because he taught me that anything can happen if you believe and think positive thoughts.

—ADRIELLE CHEW, FIFTH GRADE

❖   ❖   ❖

Robert Gamez introduced me to Nelson and Kerri Fujiwara, both schoolteachers in Texas who became close friends during my year on tour. I invited Nelson to travel with me to a couple of events (including the U.S. Open), and Kerri asked me to speak to her fifth-grade class during the Valero Texas Open. That turned out to be a far more nerve-racking experience than the dozens of television interviews I'd done or my countless live national radio broadcasts.

Kids tend to cut through the clutter and get right to the heart of the matter. Evidence of this is in the essays Kerri's students wrote after my visit. Allison Yelvington wrote: "I learned a little about cerebral palsy and I already knew a little. One thing I knew was that people with disabilities aren't any different. My brother has a severe case of cerebral palsy and can't walk, talk, and has mental problems. After listening to D.J. I felt like I could do anything. He knew he could do anything and wouldn't get discouraged. That, not his disability, made him different. I think meeting D.J. was a great experience and will affect the rest of my life."

The note from ten-year-old Faith Goan brought tears to my eyes: "Reflecting on the lesson that we did yesterday, the lesson was about one man who had cerebral palsy and no matter how different he was, he let nobody bring him down. I too have dreams and here is how I reflected on yesterday's lesson.

"I am a girl who has eczema, and not many of you have it. It's not contagious and it doesn't make you feel sick. It just makes your skin very itchy and dry, and, no, it's not like chicken pox; it's better than chicken pox. When people ask me what's wrong with my skin, I don't mind telling them. It's just that I don't like it if their reactions make me feel bad. Even though my skin doesn't look perfect, I am just like everybody else. My dream is to find a cure for eczema, and I want to make my skin beautiful."

The questions I got from these kids were just as compelling as their essays.

"Do you feel sad when people point at you?"

"Not at all," I said. "I understand that I walk different from everyone else, so I expect people to notice."

"How do you get in the bathtub?"

"Very carefully."

"What do you do when you fall?"

"Well, I get back up and keep on going."

A lot of the professional golfers have had to get up after a fall, none more so than Stuart Appleby, the man I had the privilege of following in the U.S. Open.

When we met right before the U.S. Open at Torrey Pines, Stuart had just turned thirty-seven and looked like he could still hold his own on the Australian Rules Football field, the sport he played as a kid. "The best part of football was the team, the team atmosphere, and being part of that sort of environment," he said. "I'm a loner by nature, but that aspect of it was something I missed. I would come home and watch matches every now and then."

With a square jaw, blond hair, and sideburns that look like something on the *Sonny and Cher Show*, Stuart could have come straight out of central casting. Even his Australian accent fits his persona like one of his athletic-cut dri-FIT shirts. He would blend into the latest James Bond film like he'd been there all along. He also seemed to be on top of the world: eight career tour victories, a near miss in the 2002 British Open where he lost to Ernie Els in a playoff, a spot in the top thirty in the World Golf Rankings, and a mischievous smile that infects everyone who comes into contact with him. A stranger would have never guessed that Stuart had endured a blow that might have crippled lesser men, a devastating tragedy that rocked the golf world almost a decade to the day before the Open arrived in San Diego.

I didn't ask Stuart about his first wife, Renay. The subject wasn't taboo; he would have answered any question, just as he had with phenomenal grace for ten years. She had been his partner in life as well as in the insular sport they shared. "Golf was always very much like me," Stuart said. "It's a loner sport, and I like doing things myself; I like the solitude of the golf course, the mental test of it."

It seemed perfect that he would choose a golfer as his partner. Renay was a fierce competitor who gave as good as she got in her many head-to-head battles with Karrie Webb and Rachel Heatherington in Australian women's golf. A scholarship holder at the Australian Institute of Sport, Renay won the South Pacific Women's Classic, among others. She was considered an up-and-comer in Australian women's golf.

She met Stuart when she needed a 2-iron reshafted. Her local pro gave the club to Stuart, who, at the time, was a dairy-farm kid making ends meet by doing club repair. When Stuart returned Renay's club to her, he declared her to be cute, sassy, and too much of a flirt for his liking. She thought he was a too-gorgeous-by-half snob. They married three years later.

Renay caddied for Stuart on the Nationwide Tour and was on the bag for his first two American professional wins in Monterey and Sonoma. She also handled the travel arrangements and acted as rental car navigator in the pre-GPS days. They were as close as any couple in golf. When he made it to the big tour, she was there for every step, never pulling punches—"You're putting bloody terrible!"—and never losing faith. "Stuart's playing so good he's about to win," she said after he'd missed eight cuts in a row. He then won the Honda Classic and Kemper Open.

Just before they were to leave for the 1998 British Open, Renay played golf at Isleworth in Orlando with her friend and fellow Australian Jody Adams. It was her first round in months, and she shot a 75, which prompted Jody to say, "Renay, why don't you try to play the tour?"

"I couldn't be happier with my life just the way it is," Renay replied.

A week later, right after Stuart missed the cut in the British Open at Royal Birkdale, the two were standing outside London's Waterloo train station. They'd just gotten out of a cab and were headed to their train—London to Paris, a second honeymoon of sorts since their first one had been to a Nationwide Tour event in Boise.

Nobody saw the backup lights. It wouldn't have mattered if they had; it all happened so fast. The car reversed at a high rate of speed, pinning Renay against the front bumper of another car. Stuart was right there with her, but there was nothing he could do. She died before the ambulance could reach the hospital.

Stuart had always called her "first prize in the raffle of life." So it was fitting that the final line on her black granite tombstone (a cut she'd just picked out for their kitchen counter) was a quote from Stuart: "My best friend forever."

It wasn't easy, but Stuart pulled through, and he came out stronger. When his good friend Payne Stewart was killed in a plane crash in October 1999, Stuart was one of the first to arrive at Payne's home to be with his wife, Tracey, herself an Australian, and their children. Stuart became a source of strength to

Tracey and the kids, and an example for the rest of the tour in the way he handled the tragedy.

By the time we met, Stuart was remarried, and he and his wife, Ashley, had two beautiful daughters, with another child due in the fall. "I enjoy being a dad," he said. "I'd love to have more time with the kids. I used to drive motorsports stuff, fast cars were my thing, but my days at the track are gone now. Not with the kids. Now I enjoy sitting by the pool during the summer, just hanging out, being a bit more of a family man.

"My parents were good role models for me. What I see in myself, and the things that I have today, all came from what I learned from my father on the farm. Both my parents were critical to putting me where I am today. Now, being a father, I understand that's a role that I've got to take on, to be the kind of person my kids can look up to and try to emulate to some degree.

"The kids come out with us just about every week of the year. We're about to go three weeks in a row without them, but that's very rare. Most of the time, they're with me every week. I'd say we're one of very few families that travel full-time."

They weren't in San Diego, simply because it was a long way for five-months-pregnant Ashley to fly with a three- and a two-year-old. Plus, Stuart historically played terribly in the U.S. Open. In eleven appearances, he'd missed seven cuts. His best finish was a tie for tenth way back in 1998, just a month before Renay's death.

"In the U.S. Open, there's not that much preparation you can do because the rough's really thick so you just have to hack it out," he said. "It doesn't take that much skill. The U.S. Open's probably the hardest physical test. Augusta is one of the toughest mental tests; it's such an amazing place. The other U.S. Open courses don't hold nearly the mystique that Augusta does, but I think the U.S. Open is the toughest. They're looking for par to be the score. The demands on shot making are very, very high."

He rose to the challenge at Torrey Pines. With

Nelson Fujiwara and me dutifully in tow, Stuart had four birdies and two bogeys in the opening round and was tied for fifth when the sun set on the Pacific.

Friday was another glorious Southern California day: slightly overcast and breezy but perfect for golf. Even so, Stuart got off to a rocky start with a bogey on the first hole. Then he settled into his round and made six consecutive pars before picking up two birdies on the eighth and ninth holes. Making the turn, he was 3 under for the championship and atop the leaderboard. The back nine began with back-to-back bogeys on eleven and twelve, but he righted himself with a birdie at thirteen. Then he made a 45-foot putt for birdie on the final hole to finish at 3 under for the championship. As he walked to the scorer's trailer, Stuart was somewhere he'd never been before: leading the U.S. Open after thirty-six holes.

Yes, it was round two, but I was still a nervous wreck watching the leaderboard. After the round, Stuart turned to me and said, "You're my lucky charm. I'll see you tomorrow."

That's when it hit me: Oh my, I'll be following the leader of the U.S. Open.

The week had gotten off to a shaky start for Nelson and me. USGA officials weren't up to speed on my journey, so the credentials I got did not provide for inside-the-ropes access or entry into the media center. While I never hung out in the media tents when I had nothing to do, being able to sit through the interviews and have access to the databases was an important part of the job. Thankfully, the USGA relies on staffers from the PGA Tour to help operate their event. One of those staffers, Guy Schieppers, went to Craig Smith, director of communications for the USGA, and said, "Look, this kid is legit. He needs media credentials." Craig said, "Of course," and we were set up.

Still, U.S. Open crowds were different, especially around the final groups. Nelson and I stayed up with Stuart's group, sometimes heading to the green so we didn't miss a shot, but I realized what he'd meant when he'd called the U.S. Open the toughest test, physically. Walking through USGA rough, working to stay ahead of the throngs of people in the gallery, and doing everything possible to remain inconspicuous so as not to distract anyone were monumental hurdles.

I didn't get in Stuart's way, but Torrey Pines did. It started with a 4 putt, one of the most debilitating hammer blows a golfer can experience. Three putts are tough enough—you walk onto a green with a putt for birdie and walk off having made a bogey—but a 4 putt is like shooting off your big toe. You think you might make birdie, par at the very least, and you leave having made a double bogey. It's psychologically crippling and doesn't do much for your score, either.

Things went from bad to worse. Stuart didn't make one birdie putt, and made six more bogeys on the day. When the dust settled, he'd shot 79 and blown any chance at winning his first major.

Sunday, Father's Day, wasn't much better. His putter abandoned him, and if he missed a fairway or a green it usually meant a bogey. Stuart finished with a 75 and went from leading after thirty-six holes to finishing tied for thirty-sixth at the end of play. Still, he remained upbeat and positive despite the disappointment.

"I don't have a real job," he said. "It's an amazing life, a great life, really. Yeah it's frustrating, but it's great."

The tournament didn't end on Sunday. Unlike any other tournament, if the U.S. Open ends in a tie after seventy-two holes the USGA has an eighteen-hole playoff the following day. All the majors used to settle their championships this way, but the other three, the Masters, British Open, and PGA, abandoned the Monday finish and went with either sudden death or aggregate three- or four-hole playoffs on Sunday. But the USGA is nothing if not old school. They kept their eighteen-hole Monday playoff and show no signs of changing it in the future.

The playoff at Torrey Pines would be between Tiger Woods and Rocco Mediate, an epic battle that would go down as one of the greatest in the history of the game. Thankfully, I was able to see it. At first, no one seemed to know whether or not the playoff was an "official" round. My task was to walk every official round of the year, so it was a pretty important question.

"We should do it just in case," Nelson said after it became obvious that we weren't going to get an answer before the playoff began.

"Yeah, but we're going to be fighting thirty thousand people," I said. The gates had opened at seven A.M. and within minutes the grandstands behind the eighteenth green were full, even though the players didn't tee off until nine.

"This is a once-in-a-lifetime thing," Nelson said. "You don't want to miss it."

He was right. We walked ahead of the players to beat most of the crowds and stay out of everybody's way. Admittedly, we didn't see many of the shots, but we were there when Tiger won it. We both felt we'd been there for history.

I didn't fall a single time at the Open. But if I had, I would have gotten up, dusted myself off, and kept moving. Stuart Appleby's fall was much harder than anything I've ever experienced, but I understand the mind-set he employed to fight through his grief and pain and press forward with his life and career. Renay would have demanded nothing less.

Everyone falls. It's how you get up and move on afterward that marks the kind of man you are. In that regard, there are few men better than Stuart Appleby.

CHAPTER ELEVEN

"THE IMPORTANCE OF WHAT WE DO"

B y the second half of the season I was a veteran—
I felt as comfortable on tour as I did at home. It's
easy to reach that point when you live at golf tournaments forty-six out of fifty-two weeks. St. Louis,
Milwaukee, Moline, Memphis, Madison, Oakville,
Akron, Bethesda, Birkdale, Southport—all places
I'd never been before that felt like a faded old shoe
the minute I saw the green grass, gallery ropes, and
grandstands. I loved being a golf roadie.

As the year rolled on, volunteers began to know

who I was before I arrived. Not a week went by when I didn't sign autographs and give a handful of interviews. The caddies made me an honorary member of the Tour Caddie Association, and players brought me into the fold, ribbing me and playing games that marked me as a member of the family. At the Travelers Championship, Steve Marino and I got into a silly contest to see who took more steps in a round. Steve and I, along with his caddie, Mattie, had on Accusplit pedometers as part of a promotion sponsored by *Men's Health* magazine. By the time we got to seventeen, Steve was pacing around every tee box to get his step count up, and Mattie stepped off distances twice and took the long route to the water coolers. I still beat them.

Sometimes the galleries were the straight men for our inside jokes. When I followed Rich Beem at the AT&T National, he went sixteen holes without making a birdie, so when he finally rolled one in on seventeen, I waited behind the green and said, "It's about time you made a putt." Rich replied with, "Hey, I don't care if you are crippled, I'll come over there and whip your butt." Fans were understandably aghast. Rich and I laughed about it the rest of the year.

The following Friday night in Davenport, Iowa, Rich and I had dinner and a couple of drinks, so during his round on Saturday, he turned to his playing partner and, in a voice loud enough for every patron in lob wedge range to hear, said, "See that guy with the wooden leg? He drank so much last night I think the thing's hollow. If he gets near you, see if you hear it sloshing." Again, fans gasped in shock.

Rich knew his best line would get him in hot water, so he pulled me aside and said, "I've got a new nickname for you. From now on, you're the Pimp with a Limp, 'Pimple' for short."

Some of the ribbing was a little gentler. Olin Browne asked me for a month when I planned to follow him. At one point he chased me down the cart path and shouted, "Hey, you! I see the deal. I've got to play with some superstar for you to follow me, huh? Is that how you roll? I'm not good enough. *Nooooo*. I've got to get paired with a hotshot to get on your radar."

Those same guys who ribbed me and called me "Pimp with a Limp" went out of their way to help me when I needed them. Rich gave me one of his player guest passes to the British Open so my mother could be with Dad and me in England. He even hand-delivered the ticket an hour before his Thursday tee time despite concerns about a nagging wrist injury. Three hours later, Rich withdrew after only nine holes. The wrist was hurting too much, and he was 11 over par. But he hadn't forgotten Mom's ticket.

Later in the year, after Kenny Perry and I became close, I asked him if he would mind donating a couple of gloves, maybe a golf ball or two, to a silent auction to benefit United Cerebral Palsy. He gave me five signed gloves, three signed hats, a dozen balls (all signed), a driver that he autographed later, as well as the golf bag his caddie carried when Kenny won the Memorial and the Buick Open. The UCP sponsors were stunned. "Don't be," I said. "That's the kind of man Kenny is."

The same could be said for most of my tour player friends. When my old buddy Neil Como asked me to play in his charity tournament in Massachusetts for the Holyoke Medical Center Birthing Center, I said, "You want me to see if Robert Gamez can play?"

"Are you kidding?" Neil said. "That would be fantastic!"

I called Robert and he said, "Sure, I'd love to play." He waived his normal appearance fee and cleared his schedule.

It wasn't just players who showed extraordinary kindness and generosity, though. At the Stanford St. Jude Championship in Memphis, my pal Neil was presented with a handmade caddie bib from the patients at St. Jude Children's Hospital. On the cloth plate where the player's name goes, tournament officials had embroidered, "D.J.'s Caddie."

Neil also got the ultimate video game experience when execs at FedEx invited us to the home office to play with their multimillion-dollar flight simulator. Okay, they actually asked me to speak at their business symposium, but a little left-seat time in the simulator with a couple of tour players, Martin Laird and

Kevin Stadler, came with the deal. Neil and Kevin actually made a couple of landings; I flew us into the top of the Eiffel Tower.

I tried to do my part. After the fun and games, I visited St. Jude's, where my message was simple: There are a lot of things in life you can't control, but nobody can take away your spirit. Fight to get better, fight to live your dreams, fight every day, and never give up.

It was a message I repeated as often as I could, and one I hope to repeat for as long as I live.

"I can't tell you how much what you're doing means to me," Ken Duke told me after he'd qualified for the FedEx Cup playoffs. Ken was one of those hardscrabble grinders who learned to play the professional game on the Nationwide Tour before breaking out on tour with two runner-up finishes and a flurry of top tens.

"When I was growing up, I was diagnosed with scoliosis in my spine," he said. "I thought I was just slump-shouldered. It was just more comfortable for me to be sort of hunched all the time. Then, when I was in the seventh grade, I got the diagnosis. I wore a body cast for a couple of years. I took it off for practice when I was playing other sports and put it back on as I was growing.

"At the end of my ninth-grade year, doctors told me I had to have surgery. I didn't know what that meant, but I thought I was probably done playing sports for the rest of my life. I figured I was done with everything. In February of 1985, I had a Harrington rod inserted into my back. It's a sixteen-inch rod, so it was major back surgery.

"That's why I appreciate what you're doing so much. I've never taken a day out here for granted. I don't know how long I'm going to be able to keep playing; I don't know how long my back will stay up. It's a touchy situation. It's tough. I see you and I think about that fear I had when I was younger, not knowing if I was ever going to play football or basketball or golf again. I'm thankful to be out here. I'm thankful every day."

Now that my season is over and I've returned to something resembling a normal life, I'm peppered with questions about the players I got to know. Fans want to know what tour players are really like and who the genuinely nice guys are. After spending a year with them I can say that, as a group, PGA Tour players are a special breed of athletes. No tour player has been suspended for drugs; no one's been arrested for battering a girlfriend; no golfer has shot himself in the thigh in a nightclub; nobody has choked a coach or gone into the stands to fight a fan or been implicated in a financial scam. Some say golf is boring. Well, if being a model of character makes you boring, then color me dull.

These men have egos, sure. They make ten-foot putts for a living. You don't do that if you aren't supremely confident in your abilities. But they also have their priorities in order, and they understand their role in the world.

"I've been to Walter Reed several times and spent time with those superstar Americans," Davis Love said to me one afternoon after finishing his round. "The thing that impresses me most about them is that they aren't mad about their situation. They know they're doing a great thing for their country, and they want to go back and do it again. Most of them feel like, hey, we were doing a good job and we want to go back and finish it. I met one guy who'd been over in Iraq, got blown up, came back, rehabbed, went back to Iraq, got blown up again, rehabbed again, went back a third time, got blown up again, rehabbed a third time, and now he wants to go back again. Some people think that's crazy, but when you see somebody with that much purpose, who believes that passionately in what he's doing, you realize what's important in life. You would think that as soon as you got hurt you'd say, Okay, I'm out and I don't ever have to do this again. They don't think that way. They feel like they're serving their country and doing what they're supposed to be doing in life. They're good at it, and they want to keep doing it.

"The positive attitude those servicemen display is just unbelievable. No matter how extensive their injuries—and some are pretty bad—they are optimistic about the future. It makes it a little easier to go out there and play golf when you know you don't have to deal with much compared to them.

"It puts life in perspective, especially out here. The one thing you learn pretty quickly as a tour player is that the big reason we're successful is the charity work we do and the good we're able to bring to communities. Sure, we can play for a lot of money, but we're doing a lot of good. The importance of what we do isn't seen while the tournament's being played. It's seen when a hospital gets a critical piece of equipment that they wouldn't have been able to afford, or a Habitat for Humanity house gets built with money the tour helped raise. That good we do trickles down to our hometowns where we might not be playing for money, but we still use our golf, our platform, to help other people. I think a couple of years ago the PGA Tour got to a billion dollars that's been given away to charity. That doesn't count what each tour player has done in his own hometown, through foundations or personal charities. I'd guess that's probably another billion dollars. It's pretty incredible. It's a great culture that the tour cultivates.

"This is what we do. This is who we are. It's what we're about. The most important thing is giving back. That's what these tournaments were founded on and what we're charged with continuing to uphold. I'm proud to be a part of it."

Those words rattled around in my noggin like a pinball, and for good reason. When I'd started this journey, it had been for selfish reasons. I had a goal and a dream, and I'd figured out a way to make it happen, but it was all about me. Sure, I'd promised to give interviews, sign autographs, and be an ambassador for all that was good and right with the PGA Tour but I'd also put my goal of walking every round on a higher shelf than everything else. Davis reminded me that the tour existed not to pamper and enrich its players (though it does that), but to make things better one charity at a time, and to remind people why we love sports and sportsmen.

I remembered that message when Kerri Fujiwara asked me for a favor the week of the WGC-Bridgestone Invitational in Akron, Ohio. A friend of her family had a daughter with cerebral palsy, and the little girl was about to undergo the same surgery I'd had to clip my adductors. While I was too young to remember the procedure, I understood the anxieties of a child fighting to be one notch closer to normal, and I knew the frustrations of a nimble mind trapped in an inert body.

"Would you mind coming up to visit her?" Kerri asked. "I think it would mean a lot to her."

It was an hour from Akron, but I would have gone much farther to help a child in need. It was the least I could do.

We met in the home of Kerri's sister, Ginger Wilczak. The young girl didn't make much eye contact, which isn't unusual for those with CP. She didn't have to look at me to communicate. When I explained who I was and what I was doing, I could see the surprise on her face. She'd seen news coverage and clips on the United Cerebral Palsy Web site about my journey.

"You know, I didn't do this to be famous," I said. Of course, I'd actually done it to live out a personal sports fantasy, but that thinking had evolved over time. "I did it to show little girls just like you that you can do anything if you stay positive and keep working. Without people like you, what I'm doing doesn't mean anything. Do you understand?"

She nodded with a glisten of moisture in her eyes.

Then I surprised myself by saying, "I'll walk a thousand miles this year, but that won't be nearly as impressive as the first ten feet you walk after this surgery. So keep trying. Don't let me down."

CHAPTER TWELVE

TOUGH DAY

Some men weep for what they've done, others for what they haven't. On Sunday, November 9, I wept for what I was about to do. It was a perfect day for golf: cloudless and warm with a hint of a Florida breeze to remind you why Disney World is America's most popular family resort. I was up early, even though my player for the week, Jason Gore, was in the top ten and didn't tee off until late morning. Still, it was going to be a busy day. An ESPN crew would follow my every step, and they wanted some additional interview material prior to my going out, but it would have been a tough day with or without them, because it was the last.

This was it. My journey would come to an end in sight of Cinderella's Castle next to a row of hedges shaped like Goofy, Mickey, Minnie, and Donald. I could think of no finer place to call it a year. The week had been perfect: zero falls, fifteen sports drinks, five bottles of water, and twenty-eight miles walked. Even so, by Sunday morning I was physically spent and running on pure adrenaline. Overwhelming emotions can have that effect.

Until that moment I'd never been able to wrap my brain around what the word "bittersweet" means. I'd always thought it had to be one or the other, sort of like the line, "It was the best of times, it was the worst of times." Come now, Mr. Dickens, it can't be both. Well, as it turns out, things can be the best and the worst, bitter and sweet, simultaneously wonderful and heartbreaking. That was my Sunday.

My goal had been accomplished. I'd walked every round of every official event on the PGA Tour calendar: 3,256 holes, 1,000 miles of walking plus another 80,000 miles of travel. I drank a total of seventy gallons of water on the courses and burned approximately 350,000 calories. I also fell twenty-nine times, an average of one tumble every week and a half. But my feelings were more than the sum of the numbers. I'd conquered my Everest, won my marathon, and, in the process, made more friends in a year than most people collect in a lifetime.

It wasn't always easy. Rain delays were the toughest. At the PGA Championship we had to walk thirty-two holes in one day, which was a hard jaunt on a difficult golf course. Other times I walked a full thirty-six. That was, literally, like running a marathon. But as the year rolled on and my conditioning improved, my recovery times quickened. Sometimes I just needed to sit down for thirty minutes to catch my second wind. Other times a one-hour power nap did the trick. Of course, sometimes the nap stretched for two, three, or four hours. Once in Akron I lay down after my round for a quick nap and slept all afternoon and night, waking at seven the next morning on top of the covers and still wearing the previous day's clothes. Most of the time a quick nap—five minutes in the car between the golf course and the hotel—was enough to recharge the batteries.

The most difficult part of the final weeks wasn't the physical toll; walking twenty-five to thirty miles a week had become my normal routine. It was the fact that I had so many players wanting me to follow them and so little time left. In the final month, a dozen players came up and said, "I hope you get to follow me" or "If we don't hook up this year, please put me on your list early next season." I didn't have the heart to tell them that this was a one-year deal. Boo Weekley even said, "Tell me how much it'll cost to have you do this again next year and I'll make sure you get the money."

That elixir added a tinge of bitterness to my sweet, sweet ending. I'd gotten so close to the players and their families, intertwining myself with the fabric of tour life, that the thought of not showing up at the media center on Wednesday, not hearing the standard "Whassup, Deej?" from so many of the caddies, and not leaving on Sunday with my standard "See you next week" made reaching the finish line seem like a letdown. I guess the old adage is true: The joy of life lies in the journey. From the beginning, I thought I would be ecstatic when I walked away from that final hole and said, "I did it." Now I wanted somebody to extend the season.

My parents were there for my final round, walking hand in hand as Jason Gore had three birdies, one bogey, and a double bogey to post a final-round score of even par, good enough for a tie for sixteenth. "I think it's awesome what you've done," Jason said afterward. "It's kind of a dubious honor being the last guy of the year. I guess you were just looking for somebody to fill out your dance card."

"No, I specifically asked for you." Jason had actually sent me an e-mail several weeks before. He'd read the blog and wanted to be part of the experience.

"Well, thank you," he said. "I have, indeed, read your blog since early in the year, and you're a great writer. I think it's fantastic."

I will remember those words for the rest of my life, as I will many of the memories from my incredible year. I'll never forget Phil Mickelson coming up to me in the parking lot at Oakland Hills and saying, "I've been reading about what you're doing and I think it's a real inspiration. Keep up the great work." And I'll always remember the way David Duval opened up to me in Atlanta about his family and the way his priorities have changed. "The commitments that came with being the number-one player, I never quite got," he said. "One day I woke up and was ranked number one, and suddenly I was supposed to be the authority on everything and the figurehead of the game. It made no sense to me, so I probably didn't handle it as well as I could have. Now, for me to marry into a family with kids and then have a couple of others, it's a pretty neat time. It so overshadows anything that goes on professionally."

And I'll never forget the many surprises I received, like the plaque the tour made for me with the photos of all the players I followed, or the many signed flags and personal mementos I was given along the way. I'll always cherish the countless conversations I had with the greatest golfers in the world, people I will know as friends for as long as I live.

Rich Beem had my family over to his house the Wednesday of Disney, where he grilled steaks and we laughed about all the things that had happened throughout the year. I told the story of renting a house one week with Robert Gamez's caddie, Mark Huber, and invoking what I called the Gimp Rule. "Their master bath had the only walk-in shower in the house, so if everybody wanted to be on time, I needed the master," I said. "Small price to pay, I think." Rich got a huge kick out of that.

"What are you going to do now?" Rich asked.

"Well, I'm going to Q-school to watch Robert Gamez, and I promised an old college buddy who's the tournament director at the Merrill Lynch Shootout that I'd come down to Naples for that. I haven't decided if I'm going to Tiger's event in California yet."

Rich shook his head and laughed. "You just can't stay away, can you?"

"Not if I can help it."

And on it went. I got hugs and handshakes, kisses and congratulations while spending most of my time fighting back tears and trying not to think about what it was going to be like not to have to worry about the calluses on my toes or how my back was going to hold up next week. The ESPN guys asked me what that final walk was going to be like, and, until I made it, I really had no idea. All I could say was, "Tough day. That's going to be a tough day."

When it finally came, it was and it wasn't. The joy and love I felt from my friends made it one of the happiest days of my life; the fact that I couldn't bottle it up and keep it with me forever made it not quite sad, but certainly emotional.

Rich summed up what everyone felt when he said, "You know, when you first came out here I thought of you as the handicapped guy doing the walkabout. After a few weeks I just thought of you as the guy walking every round of the year, and by the middle of the season I just thought of you as D.J., my friend. Now that's the only way I'll ever think of you. What you did here was fantastic. But who you are is what's really made this year special."

When 1948 Masters champion Claude Harmon was on death's door in a Houston hospital, Ben Hogan sat at his bedside and said, "Claude, I just want you to know that you're probably the best friend I ever had."

Harmon replied, "Well, hell, Ben, it's a short list."

I don't have that problem. My list of friends is long and distinguished. From my parents to the people who sponsored my journey to the people who encouraged me every week by walking up and shaking my hand, I was able to accomplish my goals because of the strength I drew from others. They were the friends who walked with me every step of the way. And if my story can help someone else reach a little higher, run a little faster, try a little harder, or stick with it a little longer, then every step I took will have been worth it.

Keep moving. Never give up. You can do it. Don't let me down.

Golfers D.J. Walked With

Boo Weekley	Mercedes-Benz Championship
Brandt Snedeker	Sony Open in Hawaii
Shaun Micheel	Bob Hope Chrysler Classic
Bob Tway	Buick Invitational
Jeff Quinney	FBR Open
Chris DiMarco	AT&T Pebble Beach National Pro-Am
Lucas Glover	Northern Trust Open
Aaron Baddeley	WGC-Accenture Match Play Championship
Mark Wilson	Honda Classic
J. J. Henry	PODS Championship
Kenny Perry	Arnold Palmer Invitational Presented by MasterCard
Heath Slocum	WGC-CA Championship

Mark Calcavecchia	Zurich Classic of New Orleans
Briny Baird	Shell Houston Open
Bubba Watson	The Masters
Jerry Kelly	Verizon Heritage
Robert Gamez	EDS Byron Nelson Championship
Zach Johnson	Wachovia Championship
Jason Bohn	The Players Championship
David Duval	AT&T Classic
Jim Furyk	Crowne Plaza Invitational at Colonial
Jonathan Byrd	The Memorial Tournament Presented by Morgan Stanley
Paul Goydos	Stanford St. Jude Championship
Stuart Appleby	U.S. Open
Steve Marino	Travelers Championship
Kevin Streelman	Buick Open
Rich Beem	AT&T National
Peter Lonard	John Deere Classic
Sean O'Hair	British Open
Carl Pettersson	RBC Canadian Open
Jason Wagner	WGC-Bridgestone Invitational

Stewart Cink	PGA Championship
Davis Love III	Wyndham Championship
Ken Duke	The Barclays
Martin Laird	Deutsche Bank Championship
Ben Crane	BMW Championship
Fred Funk	Viking Classic
Dudley Hart	The Tour Championship Presented by Coca-Cola
Woody Austin	Turning Stone Resort Championship
Chez Reavie	Valero Texas Open
George McNeill	Justin Timberlake Shriners Hospitals for Children Open
Olin Browne	Frys.com Open
Troy Matteson	Ginn sur Mer Classic
Jason Gore	Children's Miracle Network Classic Presented by Wal-Mart

ACKNOWLEDGMENTS

The problem with a book about living a dream is that it is almost impossible to thank everyone who made it happen. To avoid the risk of missing someone, I want to give an especially heartfelt thanks to all the PGA Tour players, their wives, girlfriends, and families, as well as Commissioner Tim Finchem and his entire PGA Tour staff, and all the volunteers who bring golf to the fans week in and week out.

I also want to thank Jim Nantz, Ken Venturi, the CBS Sports golf team, everyone at ESPN, NBC Sports, and *Golf World* magazine; all the tour caddies who went out of their way for me; my sponsors: FedEx, Southwest Airlines, Ashworth, FootJoy,

Canon, Accusplit, Marriott, Ritz-Carlton, and Outback Steakhouse; and Continental Airlines for providing me with air travel to the Canadian Open and the British Open. Also Jen Bergstrom, Emily Westlake, and the great staff at Simon Spotlight Entertainment for believing in this idea and shepherding it through to completion, as well as my agent, Alissa Super, and my coauthor, Steve Eubanks. Many thanks.

To my family and friends: Ann, Jackie, and Don Gregory, Dana Rieger, Lacee Collins, Anthony Hernandez, Bethany White, Neil and Cassandra Como, Jerry Krumenacker, Kelly Thompson, Doug Wells, Alyssa Grawey, Nelson and Kerri Fujiwara, the students at Meadows Elementary School, United Cerebral Palsy and their affiliates, Craig Bowman, Phil and Roger Boyer, Shane Foley, Andrea Sweet, Troy Hopkins, Maggie Milikan, Tony and Marlene Caucci, Tom Vavra, Kim Cairns, Tim Briles, Karen Elyse, Jim Gillis, Jonathan DeVito, Jay Dillard, Randy and Jen Thomas, Tom O'Brien,

ACKNOWLEDGMENTS

Bill King, Jay Darter, Preston and Mary Ann Lentz, Sunshine Through Golf Foundation, Chris Golla, Penny Cooper, Broke and Anne Lineweaver, Brian Kajiyama, and everyone who played a role—big or small—in making this incredible adventure possible, a true and heartfelt thanks.